A SCANDALOUS PEOPLE

A SCANDALOUS PEOPLE

*Ephesians on the
Meaning of Christian Faith
and Human Life*

Micah D. Carpenter

WIPF & STOCK · Eugene, Oregon

A SCANDALOUS PEOPLE

Ephesians on the Meaning of Christian Faith and Human Life

Copyright © 2020 Micah D. Carpenter. All rights reserved. Except for brief quotations in critical publications or reviews, no part of this book may be reproduced in any manner without prior written permission from the publisher. Write: Permissions, Wipf and Stock Publishers, 199 W. 8th Ave., Suite 3, Eugene, OR 97401.

Wipf & Stock
An Imprint of Wipf and Stock Publishers
199 W. 8th Ave., Suite 3
Eugene, OR 97401

www.wipfandstock.com

PAPERBACK ISBN: 978-1-7252-5775-7
HARDCOVER ISBN: 978-1-7252-5776-4
EBOOK ISBN: 978-1-7252-5777-1

Manufactured in the U.S.A.   JANUARY 14, 2020

All Scripture quotations, except for the author's own paraphrases, are from the New International Version. Grand Rapids, MI: Zondervan, 2011.

In Memory of Dean Fredrikson, a Teacher and Friend

Contents

Acknowledgements ix

Introduction xi

1: The Scandal of Particularity: Paul Among the Philosophers (Eph 1:1–14) 1

2: The Scandal of Power (Eph 1:15–23) 18

3: The Scandal of Grace (Eph 2:1–10) 30

4: The Scandal of Unity (Eph 2:11–22) 48

5: The Scandal of God's Human Project (Eph 3:1–13) 66

6: The Scandal of Love (Eph 3:14–21) 79

7: The Scandal of the Church (Eph 4:1–16) 94

8: Ethics and the Scandal of the Christian Life (Eph 4:17—5:20) 110

9: Christian Relationships and the Scandal of Submission (Eph 5:21—6:9) 128

10: The Scandal of Warfare (Eph 6:10–24) 138

Conclusion: The Meaning of Christianity and the Scandal of Christian Existence 155

Bibliography 163

Acknowledgements

I WOULD LIKE TO thank the people who read my manuscript at various stages of writing and offered some helpful feedback along the way, much of which played a role in the final shape and content of the book. These include Justin Burpo, Laura Engelstad, Mike Garry, and Mike Gutz. I would also like to thank Fred Martin, who offered me advice about the work of writing. He has also influenced me, through the example of his preaching, toward a deeper love of Scripture and a desire to voice its message to God's people through thoughtful words. Finally, I would like to thank my wife, Katie, for her constant encouragement, companionship, and support.

Introduction

Part 1: Why Did I Write this Book?

IF YOU ARE OPENING this book with the intent to read it, I believe that you are owed a brief explanation as to what this book is. This book is not a commentary, an exegetical study, or a work of systematic theology. It is a conversation. Let's sit down together, read Ephesians, strain our minds and our imaginations, and have a good chat. If you want all your difficult textual questions answered, there are many good commentaries on the shelf. This book is here to help you ask some new questions—and not just about this ancient letter, but about God, your life, and the purpose of the entire universe.

Paul's letter to the Ephesians is a work of timeless theological genius which brilliantly addresses many of the enduring questions about human life. It presents a scintillating vision of the glory of God and the meaning of Christian faith. It also brings an urgent and revitalizing message to the church in our time. The message is this: that in Christ, God has enacted a plan for the world which is most surprising in the face of its conventional rationalities and religious common-sense. God has invited us to be inhabitants of this redemptive drama through faith, and insofar as we do so, we are a scandalous people.

The idea of *scandal* figures significantly in the New Testament. The English word actually comes from the Greek *skandalon*, which refers to a sense of offense or a stumbling-block. For example, in Galatians 5:11, Paul argues that for him to preach circumcision would be to abolish the offense or scandal of the cross. It's a concept which comes across powerfully in 1 Corinthians 1, where Paul presents the cross as "a stumbling block to Jews and foolishness to Gentiles," yet God's very power and wisdom for those who believe. The word itself does not actually come up in Ephesians, but it is inescapable in our application of its message. Ephesians presents a vision of the conflict between the glorious power of God and the fallen powers of the present age, and of the surprising actions by which God has created a people and set them apart for his purposes in the midst of this conflict. The result of this can be nothing else but a people who, by their allegiance to Christ, are rebels against the world's rebellion, and therefore embrace a way of life and a kind of self-understanding which are scandalous according to the status quo. Such a people, and such a church, is not only what God wants, but also what the world needs.

As I have said, this is not a book of systematic theology, and yet it is deliberately (if not systematically) theological. Every chapter explores important questions of theology, and some chapters delve into theological reflections which (if I have been successful) are challenging and thought-provoking. But my intent has been to keep technical theological jargon to a minimum.

In some ways, this book is inspired by Karl Barth's theological commentary *The Epistle to the Romans*.[1] I say that with all due modesty, of course. Barth's commentary was revolutionary in its theological context and remains a landmark of twentieth-century theology. Of course, I entertain no illusion of imitating such a thing. But my aim in writing has one similarity to Barth's book: *The Epistle to the Romans* is not an ordinary commentary which exegetes the text and systematically explains interpretive issues, but functions as a springboard by which Barth introduced and expounded some powerful theological themes which he saw emerging from Paul's letter. I will readily own—in criticism of my own work as well as Barth's—that there are many better ways of studying Scripture than this, and I encourage you to use them. But there are many worse ways of doing theology. My intent has been to likewise explore some theological issues which are raised in Ephesians which I believe are powerfully formative, not only for our theology, but also for our Christian self-understanding and way of life.

This book is also philosophical. Ephesians raises many of the profound questions humans have asked throughout the centuries, and addresses them in surprising ways. For instance, what is the relationship between the one and the many? In other words, how do we reconcile the diversity and fragmentation which we see in the world with the intuition that everything

---

1. Barth, *Epistle to the Romans*.

Introduction

must ultimately cohere together in a single rationality? Does the history of the world have a meaningful direction? What does it mean to be human, and how do we live by that meaning in our everyday lives? What is nature of power? How has it gone so wrong in our world, and how can it be made right? Why are we as humans so divided from each other, and how can those rifts be healed? What is the meaning of love, and of human fellowship? What is a Christian view of ethics? Where do we find an adequate basis and method for fighting evil in the world? These are questions worthy of our ultimate attention, and Ephesians, in its own unique, Christ-saturated way, offers answers deserving of our reflection.

Every chapter of this book begins with a paraphrase I've written of the passage at hand. This requires an important disclaimer: I am not an expert at translating Greek, and these paraphrases should not be treated as authoritative. I urge the reader to make use of a good translation alongside it. I wrote these paraphrases based largely on English translations and partly for my own benefit, as an exercise in thinking through each passage. But I have also attempted to make them at least somewhat clarifying and illuminating. Sometimes I have broken up Paul's long sentences into smaller, simpler pieces, with key ideas and clauses repeated. I have also made a few interpretive suggestions which give some clarifying focus on the ideas in the text under discussion. Again, I strongly recommend that these be read alongside a good English translation of Ephesians.

Every chapter opens with a paraphrase and closes with a prayer. There's a note of explanation for that, too. For the past few years, I have been exploring an idea which I like to call "theology in the second person."[2] In short, this means approaching our theology not merely as an intellectual reflection *about* God, but also as a relational response *to* God. Theology originates not from a discovery we have made about God, but from a self-revelation God has given to us. Theology's proper goal is not mere knowledge about God, but a right relationship with him, expressed in all our relationships and activities. That does not for a moment remove from theology the task of logical, objective thinking, but it firmly sets that work in the context of the ongoing conversation between God and his people. The task of theology, so considered, is to listen carefully to what God has said to us, to do our best to make proper sense of it in conversation with others, and to shape that understanding toward the response to God which he desires. This response not only takes the form of personal prayer and

---

2. Carpenter, *Theology in the Second Person*.

Introduction

obedience, but is also manifest in the life of the Christian community: the church. In all our talk *about* God, we must never forget that God himself is present and interested in what we are saying. He does not want merely to be talked *about*. He wants us to turn and speak to him. As such, all true theology should be expressible as prayer, and that is what I have attempted to embody in the structure of this book. Each chapter begins with a word of God addressed to us, turns toward reflection on that word, and concludes with what I hope is an appropriate (although inevitably inadequate) response.[3]

Finally, a word about the originating idea of this book, and the man to whom it is dedicated: Dean Fredrikson. Dean was a teacher of Bible and theology for years at Oak Hills Christian College in Bemidji, MN. Although he retired before I became a student there, I had the privilege of learning much from Dean for a few years before he died. Many of the things we talked about are discussed in his book, *Creation and Creation's God: One God, One Story, One People*.[4] There he argued how Scripture "Presents a vision of ultimate reality that provides a unified account of the origin of the universe, what it means to be human, and how Jesus Christ has demonstrated true humanity in a world of change and dominant evil", and that "The personal, creator God of Genesis is still the creator God who is persistently mentoring humans to become the kind of persons who meet with his approval, in collaboration with whom he will fulfill his purposes in the creation of this world."[5] Dean was always particularly fond of the book of Ephesians, and a few months before he died, we had a conversation about what might have happened if he had written his book in the form of a commentary on Paul's letter. In some respects, this is that book. It is certainly not a rewrite of *Creation and Creation's God*, and I have not attempted to mimic it. It represents my own thoughts and viewpoints rather than Dean's, as similar as they are on many points. But my book is written in part out of the desire of a student to honor the memory of his teacher and to pass on to others

---

3. I have some inspiration in this from Augustine's *Confessions*, in which he routinely shifts between abstract theological musings and outbursts of prayerful delight in God. The two often actually merge completely together (Augustine, *Confessions*). I am also influenced by Martin Buber's *I and Thou*, in which he calls for us to adopt a posture of relational dialogue with God and one another, rather than seeing them as mere objects to be known and pondered from a distance (Buber, *I and Thou*).

4. Fredrikson, *Creation and Creation's God*.

5. Fredrikson, *Creation and Creation's God*, book synopsis.

Introduction

some of the gifts which he has received—to take up fallen seeds and plant them in new soil, in the hope of future fruit.

That is the way of life and the way in which all good things go forth. What good I have written, I leave to you, the reader, to judge. What matters is the voice of God, who has spoken glorious words to us. Let us take them up together and feast on the riches of Christ!

Part 2: Why Did Paul Write Ephesians?

So much for my purposes in writing this book. What were Paul's purposes in writing Ephesians? I have already said that this book is not going to be a textual exegesis or commentary on Ephesians, but still, Paul's letter is the subject material of my writing, and to neglect its own context would be an injustice against it, as well as to my readers. In this section, I mean to very briefly describe the lay of the land of Ephesians, and by doing so, I hope to provide some justification for my approach to the chapters which follow.

Many studies of Ephesians spend considerable time examining the history and culture of the city of Ephesus. I have not chosen to do that.[6] Although such studies are surely profitable, there is some evidence that Paul's letter in question was not specifically directed just to that city. Many scholars regard it as a circular letter, kind of like an ancient pamphlet which was sent from place to place until it had completed its intended circulation. It is speculated that Ephesus was the final destination for the letter and the last address to be inscribed on the circulation list; hence the name *Ephesians*. I myself am neither a historian nor a textual critic, so my own opinions on this matter may be worth little. But I find this a compelling hypothesis based simply on my own reading of Ephesians.

To defend this point, it's helpful to take a step back and ask another important question about Ephesians; namely, was it really written by Paul? Many scholars have doubted it. They've held Ephesians up to the light of other texts which are assumed to be authentically Pauline, and noted some significant differences, both in style and content. Gone is the intensely personal voice of the apostle passionately addressing people by name, and

---

6. At certain points throughout the book, I do make at least a passing note about Ephesus, such as that it was the home of the temple of the goddess Artemis. While, for reasons explained here, I don't want to become too fixated on the particularities of Ephesus, as a major city in Asia Minor and probably at least one of the target destinations for the letter, it really is as good a place as any to examine the original context for Paul's epistle.

present is a style of writing which is Pauline by idea but seemingly transposed into a style more lofty, more grand, more (we could say) churchly. We know based on the records in the book of Acts that Paul spent considerable time in Ephesus and sunk deep ministry roots there. Is it conceivable to think that he would write a letter to this church without mentioning a single person by name, except for his own messenger Tychicus?

But the argument for Pauline authorship is strong. It is natural to attribute to Paul a letter which begins by claiming his name. Other details point this direction as well, including the aforementioned Tychicus, who also appears to have been the deliverer of Paul's letter to the Colossians. (In fact, the two letters have more than a passing resemblance to one another in both content and tone.) Perhaps even more significantly, the theological heartbeat of the letter seems unmistakably Pauline. Here the author repeatedly emphasizes the idea of finding one's source, identity, mission, and destiny through being "in Christ." It could be argued that this idea—salvation, justification, mission, etc., through union with Christ—lies at the heart of Paul's theology. We also see powerful teachings in Ephesians about salvation by grace through faith, the union of Jews and gentiles as a single people of faith through the work of Christ, a section devoted to defending/explaining the author's apostleship, and teachings about the church emphasizing its unity and diversity with the comparison to a physical body. All these (and more could be named) seem to fasten it irremovably to the thought and mission of Paul, based on his other writings.

In sum, Ephesians emerges as a book which bears unmistakable hallmarks of Paul, yet also significant differences from his other letters; namely, a sense of lofty style as if from a higher, more generalized viewpoint, the absence of any obvious problem being confronted, and the even more conspicuous absence of personal greetings and messages. All of these pieces of evidence correspond perfectly with the circular letter theory. Here we have the Apostle Paul writing a letter to be passed along through many of the churches he knows and loves throughout Asia Minor (perhaps with Ephesus as its final destination), giving a message specific to the common needs of the time and area yet general enough to speak to everybody, probably delivered by his coworker Tychicus. It's as though Paul has penned a summative declaration of Christian belief, identity, and mission; a manifesto not only for the church in Ephesus, but for the church in all Asia Minor—and indeed, the church in all times and places.

Introduction

But what exactly is this message? It has already been hinted at in the previous chapter, and the chapters to follow will seek to explore it in greater depth and breadth. But it stands to be pointed out here that Ephesians does indeed have a message. Perhaps that is obvious—don't all books of the Bible have a message? We rightly assume so, but some of them are easier to pick out than others. When we look at many of Paul's other letters, for example, some jump out with themes that are instantly identifiable to those who have spent much time reading them, or much time in church pews where they have been preached. For example: Romans is about justification by faith, 1 and 2 Corinthians are about a laundry-list of messy first-century church problems, Galatians is an anti-legalist manifesto, Philippians is a joyful walk down the sunny side of Paul's theology, 1 and 2 Thessalonians deal with questions about Christ's return, and the pastoral epistles give instructions about church governance to young leaders in challenging situations. All of these examples, while correct in some general sense, are vast oversimplifications. Yet the point is that it is fairly easy to come away from most of Paul's letters with a sense of what they are "about," even if that sense is a bit too simplistic at first glance. But Ephesians seems a harder nut to crack. It says many excellent things, but can read like a bit of a theological hodge-podge.

That has led, in my observation, to a common approach toward reading and applying Ephesians which I find unsatisfactory. In lieu of pursuing an underlying logic to the book, Ephesians is often read merely as a source from which to draw various useful points for theology and church practice. In one sense, there's nothing at all wrong with that. If we are going to have ideas about theology and church practice—and as Christians of course we must—such ideas should be grounded in Scripture. But Scripture ought to be more than just a place from which mine our ideas. It is meant to address God's people with a coherent, living message. Too often, Ephesians in particular, as a book whose focused message often eludes us, is valued simply for its smattering of memorable and beloved verses. For example, we find great statements about election and predestination in chapter 1. In chapter 2 we find a succinct and eloquent description of salvation by grace through faith alone, as well as a moving portrait of church unity. Chapter 3 gives us a glorious statement of God's love and a stirring doxology. Chapter 4 gives us some of our favorite teachings about the church, and chapter 5 provides some go-to statements about Christian marriage. And who can

Introduction

forget the object lesson about the armor of God and its implications for spiritual warfare in chapter 6?

Again, I don't mean to dissuade anyone from quoting any of these verses, and certainly not from leaning on them for our theology and Christian living. I simply mean to emphasize that Ephesians is more than just a collection of great verses. It's a coherent book with a penetrating message for Christian belief and human life. It is this message, its philosophical underpinnings, and its implications for the life of God's people, which I mean to explore in the following chapters.

Here's a preview. In Ephesians, we find a number of profound themes interwoven together. These include the significance and blessedness of membership in God's people, the benevolent power of God in opposition to the spiritual powers of evil in the world, the unity of God's people (even in and through their diversity) which accords with the unity of all things in Christ, the power of God's love, God's church as both a people who dwell in God's eternal purposes and as God's force for enacting these purposes in the world, and the implications of these purposes regarding everyday relationships.

But these are not just random thoughts strung together. Ephesians uses first-century theological language to tell the story of God's gracious initiative to redeem for himself a holy and beloved people, drawing them out of their former identity as victims of and collaborators with the forces of evil in the world, and forging them into an army of servant love who demonstrate and manifest the wisdom of God. All of this is accomplished by the simple but profound reality of Christian faith which is somehow encapsulated in Paul's little phrase "in Christ." Jesus Christ is the one in whom the shattered world is put back together and enfolded once again into the blessed purposes of the creator. When human beings enter union with Christ by faith and the power of the Holy Spirit, they become participants in this great putting-together of all things. That is a matter simultaneously of sheer unmerited grace, and of daily responsibility to live before God as persons of faith, hope, and love in the midst of a broken world. This is but a brief summary of the ideas which will be unpacked in the following pages. The point is that Ephesians really does have a solid, unified, and vital message for its audience, whether that be the church in Ephesus, Christians living in Asia Minor, or believers throughout the world today.

Although my point has perhaps already been made, a metaphor for our practice of hermeneutics (reading and interpreting Scripture) is irresistible.

Introduction

Too often, I think, we read Scripture like we are digging in a mine and extracting various nuggets of truth buried in the text. In some cases, this means that we casually peruse the pages until something of particular interest jumps out at us. In other cases, we painstakingly dig through the text and its ancient context, leaving no stone unturned, in search of buried treasure. Neither of these practices are bad. In fact, to some extent, both may be necessary: the former as a practical reality of the growing Christian who doesn't always have hours of time in a library at his disposal, and the second as a matter of our responsibility to come to grips with the truths surrounding this amazing collection documents which has come down to us through the history of God's people and was delivered in an ancient context very different from our own. However, neither practice—which each in its own way can be called "mining the text"—does full justice to Scripture.

I suggest that Scripture should be treated less like a mine and more like a garden. Both involve hard work digging in the dirt. But whereas mining involves the stripping away of so much useless stuff in order to get certain valuable things we are after, gardening involves bringing from all the soil its good, life-giving potentiality. We aren't after dead minerals, but living fruit. We aren't satisfied just with answering the question "What can we find down in here?", but also want to ask, "What is God growing here?" Scripture is not a graveyard of buried facts, but a fountain of living truth; an orchard of fruit-bearing trees. Specifically, as we turn to Ephesians, we need to learn to see it as more than a collection of great statements to pull out and use for this and that, but as a cohesive message, intelligently and beautifully fashioned by Paul for his first-century audience and by God for his people in all times and places. The following chapters seek to examine the theological trees which are growing in Ephesians, and to see what kind of fruit God means them to produce in our lives and in the life of his church.

I believe that this is usually an appropriate perspective as we open the pages of our Bibles. We absolutely must ask the questions "What did this text mean in its original context?" and "What does this text mean now?" But we haven't done justice to the kind of thing the Bible is until we have also addressed the question "What does God want to *do* with this text in the unfolding life of his people—in their theology, their spirituality, their vocations, their relationships, and their character?" God's word is not meant merely to convey information, although it undoubtably does that. It is also meant to *do things*: to part waters, move mountains, raise the dead, and create new worlds.[7]

And that, perhaps, is a good note on which to move forward into our conversation on Ephesians. This amazing book was launched by Paul like a sturdy vessel into the stormy waters of the ancient world. It floats on into our own modern age as an ark preserving a message of timeless theological genius. But as we crack open its doors, we find ourselves beholding a new realm, in all its surprising life forms, created by God in Christ Jesus to be unleashed upon the earth. Let us enter that world which Ephesians describes, and even in the midst of our lives in this present age, learn to live as members of this new creation: God's holy people in Christ who inhabit the reconciliation of all things.

---

7. Here I invoke the theory of hermeneutics called speech-act theory, which argues that the text not only communicates information, but seeks to perform various other actions as well.

1

The Scandal of Particularity
Paul Among the Philosophers

Paraphrase: Ephesians 1:1–14

FROM PAUL, AN APOSTLE *of Christ Jesus by the will of God, to God's holy people in Ephesus, who are faithful in Christ Jesus: grace and peace be to you, from God our Father and the Lord Jesus Christ.*

May the God and Father of our Lord Jesus Christ be praised! In Christ, he has blessed us in the heavenly realms with every spiritual blessing.

God chose us in Christ before the creation of the world to be holy and blameless before him. In his love, he pre-purposed us from the beginning to be adopted into his family—royal heirs with and through his Son Jesus Christ. This was not only his purpose but also his pleasure, overflowing to the praise of his glorious grace, which he has freely given us in his beloved one. In him, through his blood, we are redeemed and forgiven of our sins. This too came of his glorious grace which he has lavished on us. In his great wisdom and understanding, God was pleased to reveal to us the mystery of his will (his purpose in Christ) which has unfolded in the appointed time of its fulfillment. This purpose was to bring all things in heaven and earth together into unity under Christ.

It is in him and for this purpose that we too have been chosen. God, who works out everything in accordance with his purpose, also pre-purposed us, his people, according to this plan. He did this so that we, who were among the first people to put our hope in Christ, might contribute to the great praise of his glory. You were included in Christ when you heard the message of truth, the good news of your salvation. When you believed, you were marked "in Christ" with the seal of the Holy Spirit. He is a deposit guaranteeing our inheritance until the time of our redemption, when God comes to claim us as his own. This too will be for the praise of his glory!

In these words, Paul breathlessly exclaims the glories of the eternal purposes of God. His prose here is like a turbulent and effervescent waterfall of delight in the great works of God. But Paul's contagious joy, which he so wants to share with his audience, is not simply over a grand theological idea about God, but a reality which has entered the world, in which Paul and his audience personally participate: the death and resurrection of Jesus Christ. Because of Jesus and what he has accomplished, Paul joyfully declares that those who put their trust in him are beneficiaries of (and collaborators in) the eternal and glorious purposes of God.

We need to be aware from the outset that these opening paragraphs of Ephesians, which at first glance might appear to us a glorious but somewhat chaotic jumble of theological phrases, are really a story. One of the basic characteristics of all stories is that they are tensed: they have a beginning, a middle, and an ending. That exactly describes the structure of Paul's paragraph here, although this may be obscured to us by the sheer scope of its timeline, which begins in eternity past, ends in eternity future, and dwells in the "now" of our history which has been punctuated by the great central event of Jesus' death and resurrection.

Like all stories, however, Paul's has a backstory. To tell this backstory, we would properly need to recite the entire Old Testament. We won't do that, of course, though I hope that you will read it yourself. We will at least need to think a little bit about the beginning—God's purposeful and loving act of creation as described in Genesis. But first, to see this passage in the prophetic perspective in which it properly belongs, we will need to begin with a different kind of backstory: the story of human thought regarding the meaning of the universe and our place in it as human beings—or in other words, the story of philosophy.

The Scandal of Particularity
The Philosophers' Quest: The Unity of All Things

The story of philosophy is all about the attempt to answer the question "What is ultimate reality?" Throughout the era of early Greek philosophy, this specifically took the form of the question "What is the one irreducible thing, substance, or concept, to which reality can be boiled down?" One of the first attempts of an answer was put forward by Thales, who speculated that all material reality was some form of water. As silly as such an answer might sound to us, the significance of Thales's proposal lies in the basic intuition that reality is reducible to some kind of unity. This same intuition continued to drive the development of Greek philosophy, from Pythagoras, who reduced reality down to numbers or mathematical ratios, to Plato, who conceived of ultimate reality as a world of forms (that is, a realm of immaterial, timeless ideals), the top of which was the all-embracing but mysterious form of the *good*. According to Plato, who has been tremendously influential throughout the history of human thought through the present day (one philosopher from the last century said, with only a little exaggeration, that all Western philosophy is a merely a long series of footnotes to Plato), humans only have contact with ultimate reality through the intellect. According to Platonism, the great good of human life is to detach ourselves from our material and temporal concerns which cloud our reason, and gaze with our mind's eye upon the immaterial and changeless world of the forms: the good, the true, and the beautiful. Put differently (and significantly for the question which we will examine in a moment), Plato and the philosophers who followed him tended to equate ultimate reality with those things which, while existing apart from the material world, are *universal* rather than *particular*. To discover the ultimate meaning of things, we need to look away from particular objects, people, and events, and look to the universal qualities which underlie them.

Certainly not all Greek philosophy took up this exact perspective, as influential as it was, but again the most important point to be seen is that almost all the Greek philosophers were consumed with the question of how to find the essential unity of all things. This has been described as the question of *the one and the many*, and can be restated as follows: "In a world which contains such a seemingly chaotic multiplicity of objects, materials, creatures, and events, how do we find an underlying unity which makes sense of them all and pulls them together into a single coherent scheme?"[1]

---

1. This question has arisen again in the form of the modern physicist's pursuit of a

If there is a *one* underneath the *many*, how does it have contact with the world? How can we understand it and order our lives accordingly?"

Perhaps no more important question has ever been posed in the history of philosophy. And lest we think that this is merely an academic question suitable only for theorists of the abstract, we should be reminded that this a question which really bedevils us all. Whenever we struggle with the sense that our world and our lives are too chaotic; when we feel that our world is broken into many pieces; that eventually things must (we hope) fall together and make sense; that we want to live our lives in a well-ordered way toward an appropriate goal—we are wrestling with the central question of philosophy, and perhaps of human life itself.

In summary, there are at least two essential questions which emerge from the study of philosophy. First, "What is the ultimate reality which gives unity and coherence to all the complexities of our world?" Second, "What is our relationship to this ultimate reality—how can we connect our life to what ultimately matters?" These are two of the most important questions we can ask about our world and our place in it.

Paul Among the Philosophers: The Great Story of Reality

Ephesians 1:1–14 is kind of a glorious theological explosion which erupts in the midst of this question and presents a scandalous answer. Of course, we don't know whether Paul had Greek philosophy in mind at all when he wrote these words. But apart from any such reference, the very content of this great passage instantly puts it into dialogue with the basic questions of philosophy, for Paul's words are luminously charged with the matters of ultimate reality.

Paul's scandalous answer is this: the ultimate reality which gives unity and coherence to all things in the world is Jesus Christ. The meaning of life, and of the universe itself, is not an "it." It is not a thing, nor a disembodied idea, but a person: God incarnate as Jesus of Nazareth, and specifically his surprising action, committed within the humble confines of time and space, of dying on a cross. Paul makes this clear: "God was pleased to reveal to us the mystery of his will (his purpose in Christ) which has unfolded in the appointed time of its fulfillment. This purpose was to bring all things in heaven and earth together into unity under Christ." And the answer to the second part of the question—how we can be personally connected to this

---

single unifying theory—a "theory of everything."

ultimate reality and thereby root our lives in something ultimately meaningful—is clear as well. God designed this whole scheme of things with us in an important role: to participate in his glory by being holy and blameless members of his family. We can do this by being united with the unifier of all things, Jesus Christ. We are "included in Christ" (and thereby become beneficiaries of and participants in the eternal purposes of God) when we hear "the message of truth, the good news of your salvation." When we believe, we are marked "in Christ" with the seal of the Holy Spirit.

Life in our chaotic world therefore has (despite appearances) a center and a unity, in which we as human beings are invited to partake. This center is the person of Jesus Christ, who has come in our history to put our world back together—a unity to mend the shattering of relationships because of human sin and rebellion. His needle for mending the torn garment is the cross, and it did its work by piercing his own flesh.

This reuniting of all things in Christ which Paul describes is also apparent in this passage in the sense that he has renarrated the history of the world in a way which is radically different from any history a human being might have documented or even dreamed up. All human events, as random as they might seem from our perspective, are enfolded into a history written by God, and therefore have a sense of direction, purpose, and coherence. It's worth taking a moment to unpack this history which we glimpse in Ephesians 1.

The Beginning

God chose us in Christ before the creation of the world to be holy and blameless before him. In his love, he pre-purposed us from the beginning to be adopted into his family—royal heirs with and through his Son Jesus Christ (1:4–5).

It is in him and for this purpose that we too have been chosen. God, who works out everything in accordance with his purpose, also pre-purposed us, his people, according to this plan (1:11).

Genesis 1:1 says "In the beginning, God created the heavens and the earth." As magnificent a statement as this is, Paul outdoes it by calling attention to God's work even before the creation of the world. When we think about this, using the word "before" to discuss events which happened before creation—and therefore before history and even time itself—seems rather contradictory. How can there be a "before" when we have stepped outside of the created world of time altogether? But we are misled if we stop merely to puzzle this out (as Augustine did, when in his *Confessions* he pondered how to respond to the question regarding what God was doing before the creation of the world). The point is that the creation of the heavens and the earth, as tremendous an accomplishment as that was, is in some sense secondary to God's primal decision to have for himself a people, united in his holy purposes through participation in Christ.

Conceived this way, we might say that the physical creation—earth, sun, stars, galaxies, and space-time itself—exists simply to provide a suitable location for God to carry out his human project.[2] God created the world because he needed some place to put his chosen people and showcase the glories of his redemptive grace on their behalf. That seems to put humankind at—or at least close to—the center of the universe. This would, of course, be a ridiculously overwrought gesture of human self-importance, were it not for two factors: first, that as shocking as this is, it was revealed to us by God himself and not thought up by a human philosopher, and second, that humans, as we see in this passage, are not at the center, though by God's grace we may be wonderfully close to it. The center is God himself.

The world is, to borrow a phrase from John Calvin, the theater of God's glory. The created universe is a stage set for a grand drama.[3] The set and the props are a means to the end of the drama (though they are included in it). The heart of the drama lies in the actors. They are not an afterthought, nor just part of the scenery. In a sense, the actors and their activities *are* the play. The roles are cast before the set is built. Yet they, the actors, are not what the play is ultimately *about*. The play is about the message which the playwright wants to communicate. In our case, the message is the praise of God's glorious grace.

God has created the world as a place for his glory—that is, the overflowing abundance of his goodness, holiness, wisdom, and love—to be made visible and celebrated and enjoyed, not in spite of his finite human creatures, but precisely in and through them. This perhaps brings us as close as we can get to understanding the mystery of what it means to be

---

2. We should make this claim with a sense of modesty, of course. We do not know the totality of God's purposes and plans for the universe. We do not even know whether or not, in such a vast cosmos, God has other sentient creatures besides ourselves who might serve a similar purpose to ours. What we do know is what God has revealed to us about his eternal purposes for us in Christ.

3. I owe much of this image of the story of reality as a theological drama to Kevin Vanhoozer in his various writings. See, for example, Vanhoozer, *Drama of Doctrine*, 35.

created in God's image; that mysterious and wonderful description of humankind in Genesis 1:26.

But if humans were created to be a mirror of divine glory, we now see that image as if "in a glass darkly" (1 Cor 13:12). The image of God remains in humankind (it must; or else God would have revoked his purpose for his people which is so greatly celebrated in Ephesians 1!). But our God-given vocation to reflect and manifest his glory has been, in the large part, neglected and perverted because of sin. The reflection is now clearly visible only in "The image of the invisible God," who is Jesus Christ (Col 1:15). He is, as we read in John 1:1–3, the word who was with God in the beginning—the word God spoke when he commanded the universe to be made. And he is also the Christ who is "slain from the creation of the world" (Rev 13:8).

In other words, the statement that "God chose us before the creation of the world to be holy and blameless" is only true when it is modified by the all-important phrase "in Christ." God's eternal plan to create a drama of glory with humans as the actors and the world as the set was *always* a redemptive drama, and Jesus Christ has always been the protagonist of that redemption. Who is God's chosen, elected image-bearer, holy, and blameless? It is Jesus Christ. To be chosen, elect, image-bearer, holy, and blameless describes the destiny to which God has called all of us, but it is only realized when we are *in Christ*; that is, when we are united through faith with him in his death and resurrection.[4]

---

4. A few words should be said here about election and predestination, which are described in this verse and this passage. Election means to be chosen, and it is frequently associated with the Reformed doctrine of individual and unconditional predestination to salvation according to God's eternal decree. It is my contention that in his writings Paul used the word-concept *election* as a deliberate extension of the scriptural theme of God's chosen people, which in the Old Testament referred specifically to Israel. The New Testament reveals, however, that being a member of God's chosen people is not mediated by membership in ethnic/national Israel, but rather by membership in Jesus Christ through faith. With this backdrop, election needs to be understood covenantally. Scripturally, to be in a covenant relationship with God has always been a twofold reality: it is a unilateral promise-act of God, but in which individuals may or may not participate depending on their faith-response. In other words, election involves a personal and free participation in a corporate, predestined reality created by God. The solidarities *Israel* and *Christ* (who is the embodiment of Israel in fulfillment of God's purposes) are that which God has unilaterally and unconditionally chosen; individuals are chosen insofar as they become members of these realities through faith.

The word *predestination* appears twice in this passage. I have paraphrased "predestined" as "pre-purposed," which I believe better conveys the sense of the word in its context with respect to modern assumptions surrounding the concept of predestination and the idea of *destiny* in general. Our impulse is to associate these terms with a fatalistic

A Scandalous People

In summary, the people of God who are "in Christ" are inhabitants of a history which is older than creation itself. They are rooted in the unity and purpose of all things, which is God's plan to have a redeemed and beloved people. Although this purpose has gotten off track, God is putting everything back together through the same Word by which it was put together in the first place. And despite the fact that our own waywardness threatens our participation in the plan, we know that Christ the lamb was "slain from before the creation of the world." In other words, God's disposition toward his people has been one of self-sacrificial redemption even before we first lost our way—and even before the creation of the world.

The End

He is a deposit guaranteeing our inheritance until the time of our redemption, when God comes to claim us as his own. This too will be for the praise of his glory (1:14)!

Let us, for the sake of closing with an emphasis on Jesus Christ as the center of history, look next at the end which Paul anticipates in this verse. That great purpose of God which he had determined before the beginning of human history will finally be consummated when this history draws to a close. Like so many statements in the New Testament, this one is marked by what has been frequently called the "already-but-not-yet." Paul here speaks of redemption and being claimed as God's own as though they are future realities we still await. But are they not already realities for God's

---

determinism, such as we can see in certain mythological stories (think Oedipus), where a character is forced to live out his or her destiny irrespective of what he or she tries to do. But in the context of Ephesians 1, predestination is explicitly personal and loving rather than an impersonal fatalistic determinism. My contention is that predestination refers to an eternal loving purpose of God, now enacted through Jesus Christ, which he had in mind even before he created the world. It is a term which stands at once in eternity past and eternity future, as it describes what God had in mind before creation and what he will fully accomplish at the consummation of all things. Individual people are, along with all creation, beneficiaries of this enacted redemptive purpose in a general sense, but full participation in these benefits are never merely a given. It requires (as we saw above in our discussion of election) personal participation through faith in Jesus Christ. In other words, all human beings have been predestined or pre-purposed by God for eternal salvation in the sense that this is the purpose God desired for them in creation, but only by responding in faith to Jesus Christ do people become personally placed into this eternal trajectory of glory. Only as such is their predestination actualized.

people, who have been redeemed by the blood of Christ and brought into the family of God? The answer is that both are true. Perhaps we could say that our identity as redeemed children of God is a present reality because it anticipates a future which is guaranteed by the invincible promise of the omnipotent God. Paul also helpfully uses the language of inheritance in this statement. An inheritance belongs to those who will receive it, even if it has not yet come into their hands. For God's people, this inheritance has been signed in the most binding contract possible: the blood of God himself in the death of Jesus Christ.

In any case, we see here that the future which Paul anticipates is in complete unity with the purposes of God from the very beginning. The apparent chaos of history and world affairs is confronted by the claim that our lives are rooted in the promise of full redemption as God's people, when God's purposes for the world and for us will be entirely fulfilled—and above all, the consummated cosmos will resound with the praise of his glory. God's desire for the world to be a participatory celebration of all his goodness will one day be fulfilled.

The Center

In his great wisdom and understanding, God was pleased to reveal to us the mystery of his will (his purpose in Christ) which has unfolded in the appointed time of its fulfillment (1:8b–10a).

You were included in Christ when you heard the message of truth, the good news of your salvation. When you believed, you were marked "in Christ" with the seal of the Holy Spirit (1:13).

In these words, Paul makes the connection between the eternal purpose of God which predates history, and the actualization of this purpose by Jesus Christ in the midst of time and space. History is filled with what seems to us chaos and uncertainty. But it is framed and enfolded by a prehistorical past and a post-historical future, both defined by the certain purpose of God.

But here we encounter a problem: how can we find a meaning in history by looking outside of history, whether before or after it? How can we look outside the world to resolve the lack of coherence within it? We live in time and space, and this is where our problems live too. How can eternity past and eternity future meet us where we live?

The astonishing claim of the gospel is that this is precisely what God has done: in the incarnation, death, and resurrection of Jesus Christ, eternity has entered time. God stepped into time and space—and not only in the sense of providence and revelation, by which he has always been relationally present in his creation. God actually became flesh and blood, at a particular place (Palestine), a particular time (the first-century AD), and in a particular bodily human being (Jesus of Nazareth). Through this action, in which the playwright stepped out onto his own stage mid-performance, God drove a nail down through the middle of history, firmly fastening it to both its purposeful beginning and its glorious end. Eternity past (God's pre-creation purpose) and eternity future (the new heavens and new earth) invaded present history and met each other at the great intersection of the cross. The time at which this happened was not random, but appointed by God, and it was through this act that God revealed the "mystery of his will." In Christ, a meaning for history, and for the all the world in all its conflicts and disparities, has been revealed and made certain. Because of Christ, we can know that God's purposes in creation are no mere myth, and that his promised future is no mere pipedream.

As we have seen above, two of the great questions about ultimate reality are "What is the unity of all things?" and "How can we personally live in accordance with this unity?" Paul's answer to the first question is found in the incarnation, death, and resurrection of Jesus Christ. It is an answer pinned to a particular event in history. His answer to the second question is that "You were included in Christ when you heard the message of truth, the good news of your salvation. When you believed, you were marked 'in Christ' with the seal of the Holy Spirit." Paul's readers can therefore connect God's great act of redemption with an event in their own lives. God's redeeming and reunifying act not only intersects with world history as a whole in the death and resurrection of Jesus Christ, but also with our personal present lives when we hear and believe the gospel. God's unifying purpose has entered the world in Christ; we become participants in that purpose when we enter Christ through faith.

The Scandal of Particularity, the Cosmic Christ, and Jesus of Nazareth

We have now seen Paul's answer to the philosopher's query as to the unity and meaning of all things in our world of so many fragmented objects, events, and experiences. The answer, in short, is the person of Jesus Christ, as the fulfiller of the creator God's purposes for his people. But we have not yet reflected the great scandal of Paul's answer.

There are many things which are scandalous about the gospel—perhaps as many reasons for scandal as there are human beings. After all, we are a species who tend to prefer solutions to our problems which are devised on our own terms, even when we are wrong. But perhaps the most confounding thing about the message of Ephesians 1 among the philosophers is what has been called *the scandal of particularity*.

Let's quickly rehearse what we said above: Paul's claim is that the meaning of the universe—the great unity of all things—entered the world at a particular place (Palestine), a particular time (the first-century AD), and in a particular bodily human being (Jesus of Nazareth). This bucks against all the instincts of human rationality. In fact, most of the Greek philosophers and those who followed them would find such a statement complete nonsense. They wouldn't even be able to follow it as far as "entered the world." According to Plato and those who followed in his legacy, it was unthinkable that the *one* would be found in our world of time and space. The *one* is not, and cannot be, physical. It is also nontemporal and therefore cannot "do things" at all. The *one*, according to the great philosophical heritage, helps us insofar as we seek to comprehend it and model our lives after its emanations of truth, goodness, and beauty, but it never reaches down a helping hand, let alone enters our world as a flesh-and-blood human being.

According to venerable philosophical traditions in both the East and the West, ultimate reality—that unifying factor which underlies everything in the world—is to be identified with universals, not particulars. For example, Plato talked about the universal forms of the good, the true, and the beautiful. Particular objects or persons may participate in these universals to a greater or lesser degree and draw on them as a source, but never the reverse. The good, true, and beautiful, according to Plato and others, do not come from a particular good, true, and beautiful being. Any such being must participate in these universal qualities which exist beyond all particularity.

But the claim of Christianity, by virtue of the doctrines of creation and incarnation, is that goodness, truth, and beauty—not to mention faith, hope, and love—are qualities deriving from the character of a personal creator God, who is a particular being. Yes, God is transcendent beyond creation as its creator, and is therefore universal in the sense that all created things universally share in the creator-creature relationship (this is indeed an essential part of Christianity's answer to the problem of the one and the many.) And it's also true that God must be thought to be beyond matter and even time as the creator of these realities. But he is not *universal* in the Platonic sense. God is not a force, an ideal of divinity, an absolute mind, a power-of-being, or sheer *being itself*. God is a person; or more accurately, a community of three persons unified as one being (we should note that the language of Ephesians 1 simply drips with trinitarian personality, as we see the great actions of the Father, Son, and Holy Spirit weave their way through the narrative of redemption). No, God is not a being beside other beings or a person among other persons, but he is not beyond being nor beyond personhood. As the creator, he is the original personal being, generous enough to create a universe of beings and at least one planet populated with persons in his image, destined for relationship with him.

God fulfilled this purpose—a community of image-bearers in relationship with him—by stepping down into his own creation at a particular time. It "has unfolded in the appointed time of its fulfillment." God fully enacted the meaning of human life on our behalf, in human flesh, and he didn't do it from the lofty dome of heaven. He did it by stepping into our own neighborhood, immersing himself not only in its "time-ness" and "space-ness" but also in its suffering and evil and death. God resolved the problem of brokenness in the world by entering the brokenness himself and being broken on the cross. He conquered death by coming to earth to die and thereby absorb death itself into "the power of his indestructible life" (Heb 7:16). And all of this was accomplished within the bodily person called Jesus of Nazareth.

This is scandalous behavior for a god. Decent, respectable gods don't get their hands dirty with the world of time and space. They don't incarnate themselves in the midst of a material, changing world. They certainly don't become human, and above all, they don't die. But the God whose glorious grace is so praised by Paul did all these things. Therefore the religion Paul is advocating (if religion is the right word for it) is an utterly scandalous one. At this point, Paul's statement from 1 Corinthians 1:18–25 is worth quoting at length:

> For the message of the cross is foolishness to those who are perishing, but to us who are being saved it is the power of God. For it is written: "I will destroy the wisdom of the wise; the intelligence of the intelligent I will frustrate." Where is the wise person? Where is

The Scandal of Particularity

the teacher of the law? Where is the philosopher of this age? Has not God made foolish the wisdom of the world? For since in the wisdom of God the world through its wisdom did not know him, God was pleased through the foolishness of what was preached to save those who believe. Jews demand signs and Greeks look for wisdom, but we preach Christ crucified: a stumbling block to Jews and foolishness to Gentiles, but to those whom God has called, both Jews and Greeks, Christ the power of God and the wisdom of God. For the foolishness of God is wiser than human wisdom, and the weakness of God is stronger than human strength.

Indeed, there have been many throughout history who have criticized the scandal of the cross, of the incarnation, and of the curious particularity of the gospel—and indeed, of God himself. These critics have emerged not only from outside the church but also from within it. There have been many Christians throughout the years who are seemingly embarrassed at the scandal of particularity and have found various ways to rationalize it. Some influenced by the tradition of Greek philosophy have insisted on reading the personalistic presentation of God in Scripture as anthropomorphism, arguing a distinction between God as he has revealed himself and God as "he really is"—which is assumed to be something more rationally respectable, such as "being itself," "the ground of being," or something like that. According to this scheme, God presents himself as an active agent in a changing world and even as being emotionally involved with it, but the rational Christian "knows better." "Surely," it is said, "the God who by all rational definition is unchanging and beyond all time doesn't respond emotionally to things which happen in the world!"

The difficulty with such a position is that, while of course our ability to know what God is really like is limited by our human finitude, the best information we have is that which God has presented to us in Scripture and in his son, Jesus Christ. If we speak of God having a shadowy, mysterious side beyond what is visible in his own revelation to us, on what possible basis can we make any claims at all about what this God must "really be like?" We are on earth and God is in heaven. We cannot search him out. Whatever knowledge we have of him is mediated to us through his own initiative to reveal himself. The best we can do is hear the word he speaks to us and believe that he is telling the truth. Our reason cannot reach beyond the limits of creation to discover hidden realities behind his word. And God is no respecter of our rational definitions of divinity.

Another (related) strategy for resolving the scandal of particularity is to invoke the concept of *the cosmic Christ*. When we puzzle over the oddness (and from one perspective, nonsense) of God becoming incarnate in a particular person at a particular time and place, we can see a possible rational solution in the idea that beyond the Jesus of history is the Christ of the faith. Here Jesus of Nazareth is interpreted simply as an emanation (perhaps one out of any number) of an eternal Christ-principle; or the *logos* (word) which we read about in John 1. In other words, Jesus Christ, in and of himself, loses his distinct personal significance, and that significance is reassigned to a cosmic force or idea, of which the historical Jesus was somehow simply a representation. According to this idea, we can read the gospels and their account of Jesus of Nazareth in such a way that their factual historicity is for the most part irrelevant. In this case, what a man named Jesus did or didn't do two thousand years ago doesn't matter, nor even whether or not he existed. The point is that we have a gospel account which, if interpreted correctly, communicates eternal principles about God, humanity, and the meaning of a moral life. Of course, not everyone who invokes the idea of the cosmic Christ principle discounts the historicity of the gospels, but such a reading does have the effect of relativizing the importance of Jesus as a figure who lived and acted in our own history.

But the real problem with such a reading is this: it distorts the fundamental essence of Christianity. Christianity (with Judaism) has never fundamentally been about eternal divine truths even if it holds critically important beliefs about them, but rather about God's specific, redemptive actions in human history. Christianity is not a pattern of religious knowledge and behavior designed to improve our lives or to lift them to a higher, enlightened plane of existence. It is not a searching out of secret divine knowledge. It is the claim that humanity is helpless to do any such thing and that God has come to us in the midst of our limitations and sinful plight. We don't need a cosmic Christ principle, we need a Christ: a Messiah. We need Jesus of Nazareth. Perhaps universal principles strike us as more rational, but what our human situation requires is a particular action of God for us, in our history, through an embodied human being. It demands the scandalous particularity of Jesus, God in the flesh, on the cross.

Of course, once we have understood this, we also need to believe what Scripture does in fact say about the cosmic Christ; the eternal logos through whom God created the world; in whom we live and move and have our being. Even if we don't pick up on Christ's role as a cosmic figure

The Scandal of Particularity

in Ephesians 1, we certainly can't miss it in Colossians 1, nor can we avoid coming to the same conclusions when we read John 1. But none of this takes away from the startling particularity and uniqueness of Jesus of Nazareth and his actions in history. The scandalous thing is precisely that this cosmic Christ, the logos, is none other than Jesus of Nazareth, and if we try to relativize him as the mere appearance of a divine principle, we shatter the claim of Christianity. Christ, whose ministry is universal as the creator and redeemer of all things, fully enacted this ministry at a particular time and place as Jesus from Galilee. To put it simply, God's ordering and redeeming activity in our universe cannot be boiled down to a universal abstract rational principle, but is to be identified with a particular person: the divine/human person of Jesus Christ.[5] Christianity does indeed have a universal scope, but in a reverse way from the intuitions of much philosophy. It is not the passive implications of general truths upon various particular things or persons in the world; it is the active transformation brought about by particular actions of a particular (divine) person, which have universal significance. They are the particular, personal, and temporal actions of God in Christ, which apply redemptively to all creation and invoke the responsibility of all persons.

Ephesians 1 calls us to extend the scandal of particularity even further. The light of God's purpose for the universe, after being focused through the lens of Jesus Christ, shines on a particular spot: God's chosen people, his church. In this passage, Paul celebrates the wonderful oddness of God's choice to use an embodied, finite, and flawed people as the vessels of his purpose in the universe. I believe that it is precisely this idea which is Paul's thesis in Ephesians, without which we will not correctly understand the epistle. Paul is telling his audience that they, God's church, are, through their union with Christ, the embodiment of God's eternal glorious purposes in the cosmos, and he goes on to explain what this means for their life together. Seen in light of scriptural history, we can identify this with what was described at the very beginning of human life in Genesis: God chose to carry out his work on earth through image-bearers, called to cooperate with him in the work of filling the world with his goodness, wisdom, and love.

---

5. This point is expounded at length by Emil Brunner in *The Mediator*.

Conclusion

Perhaps we can bring this all closer to home. All of us, in various ways, struggle with the question, "How does all this fit together?" Do our lives have a meaning? Is history going somewhere? Is there hope that the chaos in our world will be resolved, or that we will at least discover a way to make sense of it? In the meantime, how should we live? Where can we find an identity and a driving purpose to make our lives truly livable?

Whether we are aware of it or not, we as humans are adept at finding answers for these questions, even when we are not cognizant that we have so much as asked them. Frequently our answer consists merely of adaptive behaviors. We surround ourselves with projects, distractions, and amusements. We seek out the kinds of relationships which help us shore up an identity, and above all, the sense that we matter. We attach ourselves to social causes and interest groups and political parties which claim to have stock invested in matters of lasting significance. We also turn to religion. This is one of the most useful tools for scratching our existential itches. Religion promises us that if get with the right group of people, adopt the right behaviors, and recite the right creeds, we will find our answer. We use one or more of these things—entertainment, frenetic work, public causes, relationships, religion—as our interpretive key for making sense of our lives; for creating the sense that somehow how our fractured world hangs together. And if we are really desperate, we search out intellectual and philosophical justifications. We listen to the chorus of thinkers throughout the centuries who sing the praise of some grand idea which provides the unity of all things; which somehow "makes sense of it all."

Neither Paul in Ephesians nor I in this writing will give an unassailable, beyond-all-doubt answer to these questions. After all, it is quite possible that the only kinds of questions worthy of our ultimate concern are the kind which must be answered by faith—of one kind or another. But Paul certainly does offer a compelling answer; indeed, a scandalous one. This is that things in our world find their ultimate unity and meaning and fulfillment in a person—not in a profound idea, not in a noble activity, not in a grand political cause, not even in human religious devotion—but in the reality of Jesus Christ from Nazareth and the personal creator God whom he reveals and manifests. Christians believe, with Paul, that things make sense when we remember that despite their brokenness, they were all created by one loving God, a God who has promised to bring redemption, and who has brought it in his son Jesus Christ. The unity of all things is not then found in a human idea, but in the redemptive purposes of God which have unfolded in our history. What's more, we can live in this redemption, this great stitching-together of all things, by faith in Jesus Christ. We then discover that God's purpose in the world is centered around the creation of a certain kind of people: a holy people who put the riches of God's grace and glory on display in our union with the crucified Christ. In a word, participation in Christ is the surprising answer to our human quandaries.

But what does it mean to live out that strange and scandalous existence as a person—and a group of people—who are described by that dense Pauline phrase "in Christ?" What does such an existence look like? What has God done to enact and initiate it? What responsibilities does it involve on our part? That is the subject matter of the rest of the epistle to the Ephesians.

God, thank you that you have hidden these things from the learned and revealed them to little children. We are all little children before you, Lord. Thank you for confounding the wisdom of this age through the foolishness of the cross—and that in this foolishness you are willing to school us in your true wisdom. Above all, Lord, we give you thanks and praise for all that you have done as a great creator and redeemer. We thank you that in Christ, you have created us with a purpose, and that in Christ, you have redeemed us for this purpose. And what a wonderful, gracious purpose it is, Lord! You—who are glorious beyond all the splendors of earth and heaven—have called us to be a holy people of your glory. You have made us bearers of your image in the likeness of your son. Teach us, O Lord, through your Holy Spirit, to be ever mindful of what we are, of whose we are, of whence we have come and where we are going. And, giving us eyes to see the great cross-shaped path upon which we walk for your praise and honor, teach us to walk it day-by-day in the knowledge of your presence. We give you thanks and the praise and the glory, forever and ever, in the name of the Father, the Son, and the Holy Spirit. Amen.

2

The Scandal of Power

Paraphrase: Ephesians 1:15-23

I HAVE HEARD OF your faith in the Lord Jesus, and of your love toward all his holy people. Therefore, I continuously give thanks for you as I remember you in my prayers. My prayer for you is that God, the glorious Father of our Lord Jesus Christ, would give you a spirit of wisdom and revelation in coming to know him more. Then, with the eyes of your heart opened, you will know the hope to which he has called you, the riches of his glorious inheritance among all his holy people, and his immeasurably great power for us who believe—and I pray this confident that his great power is indeed at work! God put this power to work in Christ when he raised him from the dead and seated him in the heavenly realms. This realm is high above all other realms, authorities, powers, and dominions, and above every name and title which can be invoked, not only in this age, but also in the age to come. God has put all things underneath Christ's feet and has made him the head over all things. Christ rules for the church, which is his own body. The church is then the very fullness of the one who fills all things.

    Paul's first passage in Ephesians explodes with the cosmic purposes of God: eternal purposes, larger even than time and space, and yet they are purposes inhabited by this strange people who are "in Christ." That which is grandly cosmic is therefore at the same time intimately personal, as this second passage (1:15-23) reminds us. Paul turns to his audience in personal affection and gratitude for "your faith in the Lord Jesus Christ, and your love toward all his holy people." But this isn't at all out of step with the grand story of God's glory in Christ which he has just narrated. Paul is thankful that he is able to turn to his audience—friends, co-workers, disciples—and rejoice that together they are participants in this great reality of redemption which God has created in his son. They are members of this reality because of their faith in Christ, and their membership is both evidenced by and actualized in their love.

In an outburst of gratitude over this fact, Paul begins to pray for them. Notice how easily Paul moves from theology to praise to personal address to prayer and back to theology again. Although, we would rightly question whether these are really different activities at all—for Paul, or for us. Theology must explode into worship. Worship must involve us in the great fellowship of God's people. After all, the God we praise is not a solitary being, and whenever we worship him, neither are we. Worship and fellowship both must pull us into conversation with God: not merely private supplications, but as exuberantly public as Paul's prayer, which is embedded in a letter meant for a multitude. Finally, this joyful discourse with the trinitarian God, manifest in our public worship and prayer, must return to ground our theology. True theology cannot exist without corporate (as well as personal) discourse with God, for in the end, this is what our theology is. It is a logically solidified picture of a living relationship between God and his people. Theology without this lived relation is a lie. The attempt to live the relation without theology is carelessness, and that is a condition in which loving relations cannot long survive.

As we examine Paul's prayer, we could presume that there are many ways in which he might have agreeably interceded for the Ephesians. Doubtless there were illnesses and poverties and oppressions and heartbreaks of the sort which justly fill our own prayer lists. But Paul prays chiefly for knowledge; albeit modified from our typically impoverished view of knowledge by words such as *wisdom* and *revelation*. Paul's great desire for his audience, having rejoiced in their participation in God's glorious plan of redemption through Jesus Christ, is that they will more deeply know and understand this reality in which they already live. Paul's prayer is not that they will have hope, but that they will *know* the hope which is already theirs through God's calling. It is not that they will come to possess the riches of God's glorious inheritance or his great power, but that they will come to *understand* these gifts which already belong to them. We are shown here—as we will consider more closely later on—that the pilgrimage of the Christian life is one of coming to be that which we already are. It is a journey in which we learn, incrementally, what it means to live in the new country of which we are already citizens.

Kinds of Power

But Paul's greatest concern here seems to be *power*, a word which shows up four times in this passage. The reality in which Christians live—although we don't seem to fully know it, at least in an experiential sense—is the reality of the power of Jesus Christ.

This perhaps doesn't seem especially interesting to us at first glance. If we have been acquainted with the Christian worldview for any time at all, we will probably take it as a given that God is all-powerful and that Jesus, who is fully God, bears that power. We are aware of the power made visible in his miracles and especially in the salvation he has worked for us. We know that he is Lord over all and that one day all the world will acknowledge his rule. There is no need to go beyond these basic truths in our attempt to grasp the meaning of God's power in Jesus Christ in which we participate. But it is worthwhile to consider them more carefully, and to do so through greater awareness of the way in which power is integral both to our understanding of God and of human life on earth.

Perhaps we can start with a basic observation about the two meanings of the word *power* which are at play in this text. First, power is a quality, capacity, or potential—the ability to accomplish things. This can be understood both passively and actively. In a passive sense, power is mere potentiality. The man who can bench press three hundred pounds has the power to do so even while he is resting on the couch. In the active sense, we talk about power as ability in action. The man's power, which is always there whether he is using it or not, is only present in an active sense while he is lifting the three-hundred-pound barbell. In our passage, we see God's power in both the passive and active sense. Paul asserts his confidence in the *immeasurably great power of God for us who believe*. At this point, God's power might seem to be a passive fact which gives assurance of what God has the capacity to do for us. But Paul is not content merely to say that: he asserts that he is "confident that his great power is indeed at work!" He goes on to give evidence for this: we have seen God's power at work when he raised Jesus from the dead. God's power, then, is not merely a theoretical axiom about what God *can* do, but also the active reality of what God *has done*—and even now is doing.

Then there's the second use of the word power (the first was twofold as passive and active, but both forms of power refer to a quality of strength or ability): this is *power* as a concrete noun, as in an authority, ruler, or government. It's the usage apparent in our phrase "the powers that be." In this passage, we see the ultimate rule of God in Christ juxtaposed against certain "powers that be."

Power as an Attribute of God

Before we consider what this passage says about the power of God in Christ versus the powers of the world, it's worth thinking just a bit more about the nature of power itself. Perhaps it's our instinct to regard power as something bad, as an unholy temptation. After all, how many villains are there in our modern works of imagination who aren't power-crazed in some way or another? But we must remember that there is no such thing as original evil, only original goodness which has been spoiled. Evil never creates; it only corrupts. Power, like all dynamics of the created universe, is a great good which, taken out of its God-directed function, becomes a great evil.

We must remember then that power, in all its senses, is first and foremost a good attribute of God. It is expressed in our fundamental conviction that God is the creator and sustainer of all. Therefore he is able to do all things, makes active use of that ability, and must be regarded as the sovereign who rules the universe. God's rule, however, is categorically different from that of any human ruler, for whom power or authority is merely a realized possibility (and sometimes a rather fragile one) rather than a necessity (a fact inherent in the universe).

How does God use this power? A thorough answer to that question would constitute an exploration of God's character based on everything we believe he has done, is doing, and will do—in short, a review of our entire theology. But we can be more concise than that. We have already given part of the answer or at least implied it simply in reflecting on the facts that God is the creator and sustainer of the universe, and that God alone is a necessary being. This means that God didn't need to create a universe. God from all eternity is self-sufficient in the trinitarian communion of love and joy. The world was never owed its own existence. Whatever God creates is sheer gift springing from his generosity alone. To say this in more theological language, all the power at work in God's creation of the universe was an exercise of grace—or, we could even say, agape love. We have already seen in the previous passage that "in love he predestined us," and predestination may be regarded simply as the intentionality inherent in God's act of creation. God's purposes in creation—the purposes for which his great power was and is put to work—were never born out of necessity or to satisfy a need within God. They have only ever been rooted in unconditional love; the love by which God chooses to involve an unnecessary creation in the celebration of his glory. This truth (that God's power in the universe is inseparable from his love) is suggested rather tersely in this passage through the statement in verse 19 that God's power is "for us."

It may be surprising to see power and love linked together like this, being that they are often seen as strangers to each other, if not enemies. Frequently we see power in our world wielded as a force of selfishness, greed, pride, and hatred—the antitheses of love, which so often involves the surrender of personal power and control for the wellbeing of the other. But we must not ultimately keep the two separate, for two of the greatest horrors of our world are power without love and love without power.[1] We will consider this linkage between power and love again in Ephesians 3, but for now it is worth reflecting on the fact that however power is abused by selfishness in our world, and however disempowered love seems to be in the face of tyranny, the absolute power which created and governs the universe is a power of love. Or, to state this inversely, the compassionate and generous love of God for his creatures is a love which is backed up by almighty power. Such a perspective is necessary to keep us from lapsing into a sentimentalized view of God's love, as though it were merely a soft kindness and not also a warrior's blade. The other side of the coin is true, too. We must safeguard our view of God's power lest it come to be seen as the caprice of a cosmic tyrant. After all, the divine warrior's sword won its greatest battle by piercing his own flesh in stunning self-sacrifice. God's great power is, as we have already observed, power "for us." God's power is first and foremost a benevolent "power-for" rather than an antagonistic

---

1. Two images make this statement more self-evident. Consider first a tyrant who deliberately inflicts pain and suffering on his people simply so that they will be intimidated by him—power for the thrill of power. Consider second a parent being made to watch their child suffer without being allowed to provide any intervention or comfort. These are realities which are known all too well in our world, and they both invoke our outrage and sorrow.

"power-against." Whenever God yields his "power-against," he does so on the basis of that which he yields his "power-for."

Power as an Attribute of Human Agents

How do the dynamics of power, rooted as they are in the creation of the world and the character of the creator, come to play in our human life? In this passage we read not only about the power of God in Christ, but also that there are other powers present in the world: realms, authorities, powers and dominions. Clearly the point of the verse is that Jesus has power over all these, but the observation remains: there are powers in the universe other than God. That may be regarded as blatantly obvious. But it also raises perplexing questions: if God is omnipotent—that is, infinitely powerful—where is there room in existence for any power other than his own?

The answer to this question is where we first begin to see the scandal of power. In this case, it is the surprising way in which God has chosen to make use of his power: he has delegated it. He might have populated his universe entirely with passive or programmed creatures, but that evidently was not his intent. Even Genesis highlights this. One of the first things we learn about God's creation of humankind is that they are delegates of his power, made to rule in his image over the earth and its creatures. That seems like a normal enough plan for a human ruler to devise—even the mightiest king can't do everything himself. God alone can do that. But he chose not to. He wanted to involve his creatures in his rule and to share his power with them. Now, power might be basically defined as the capacity for an agent to take actions that, to a greater or lesser degree, shape the world in which he or she lives. The God who spoke matter itself into existence and shaped it into land and sea and air, gave to his human (and perhaps some non-human) creatures a small share of this world-shaping power.

Perhaps this seems like a crazy and irresponsible thing for God to do, like a parent giving her car keys to her toddler. That would be somewhat of an exaggeration, since we have already seen in the first part of Ephesians 1 how the history of the world is governed by God's unshakable purposes in creation and redemption. And yet God chose to undertake this purpose in and through created agents, which seems a risky thing to do. Once again, it is an example of God behaving scandalously. What possible purpose is there for an all-powerful, all-knowing, all-wise God to share some of his power with his feeble and foolish creatures? Surely whatever God wants to do, he can do more reliably and efficiently without creaturely cooperation.

Unless, that is, creaturely cooperation is itself what God wants. God needs no help in governing and shaping creation, any more than he needed help creating in the first place. But that which God ultimately wants to create, as we have already seen, is a *people*—not mere bodies directed by the mechanics of neural impulses, but real people, capable of personal relations and destined for faith, hope, and love. Once again, we see that God's power is inseparable from his love. He chose to make use of his power in such a way that interpersonal love (both between himself and his people, and among these people) would be possible. All real relations (and real personality) require some measure of power, which is implied in all notions of responsibility, freedom, and consent. God therefore bestowed the power of freedom (within limits) upon his creatures. Relationships, personhood, and love are simply not possible without some measure of freedom, and freedom is impossible without some measure of power.

Of course, the other-empowering enterprise of relationship implies some amount of risk. For God to delegate some of his power to other agents included the possibility that this power would be misused. This kind of risk is the cost at which all relationships are purchased. Again, it may appear scandalous to us that the God of the universe would take such a risk, and given the state of affairs in the world, we are even tempted to tell God, "I could have told you so!" We look at the evil empires, Caesars, Hitlers, and Stalins—not to mention countless little corruptions on all levels of human society—and are reminded that all these people have their power because God chose in the first place to share it. This is the scandal. God uses his benevolent "power-for" to create people. He shares some of his power with them so that they may personally participate in his good and loving rule. And then they turn and use this power against the very one who gave it to them and against each other, corrupting his loving "power-for" into self-serving, domineering, "power-against." We wonder if God's scheme of power delegation was worth it.

God's Solution to Power Gone Bad

This question, in addition to the subject we explored in the last chapter, is one of the great questions of human life, and it too can only be answered by faith. But once again, not by an empty faith, but one founded on the great action of God in the world through Jesus Christ. Through him, God has given the answer to whether his power-sharing enterprise was worth it—and it is a resounding "yes." This "yes," spoken through the redeeming work of Jesus Christ, is made audible in God's holy people: his church.

In this passage we see a twofold answer to the great problem of power gone bad. First, we are reminded that although all these realms, authorities, powers, and dominions continue to rage against God, God still reigns over them and they will one day be called to give an account to him. The power struggle between the kingdoms of the world and the kingdom of God happened at Calvary, where the former did their very worst against God's anointed one. When he went to the cross, he stepped into the center of the axis of evil: corrupt religion and tyrannical empire; sin, suffering, and death. He took all these upon himself, and in his resurrection, proved that God's power had unequivocally triumphed over them.[2]

Although these forces still shake their fists against God, Jesus rules on high, and his rule is not merely theoretical. He rules on behalf of his redeemed people, the church, and here we see the second aspect of God's answer to the problem of power gone bad. God has not by any means given up on his scandalous scheme of delegating power to his creatures. He is in the work of redeeming this enterprise in and through his beloved people. Our passage closes with the staggering statement that "Christ rules for the church, which is his own body. The church is then the very fullness of the One who fills all things." The church is the body of Christ and therefore benefits from and inhabits his power. We who are "in Christ" are participants in God's power which won its victory in Jesus's resurrection and which is therefore at work in the recreation of all things. Here we have circled back to the message of the previous section: God's promise to put the fragmented cosmos back together again is fulfilled in Jesus Christ, and God has involved his people, the church, in that fulfillment. Therefore we—feeble creatures of clay who time and time again have lost our way—have been brought by God's grace to the center of all things. God's solution to the problem of power gone bad is the power of Jesus Christ, and he has once again chosen to manifest that power in finite human beings. In other words, we might say that we, the church, are part of God's solution.

---

2. See Psalm 2, one of the great OT texts anticipating God's victorious kingdom, of which his Son is the anointed King.

Conclusion

What does this mean for Christian life? It means that we are sharers in the great scandal of power in which God wants to involve us according to his purposes. This is true in a general sense for all human beings, but in a particular and fulfilled sense for those who are redeemed in Jesus Christ. To live as a Christian therefore must involve, among other things, a return to God's intentions for the working of power in the world. There are perhaps countless specific ways this could be applied, but I see two general lessons which most deserve our attention.

First, we must consider how our own lives, reconstituted in the redeemer Jesus Christ, should bear the image of the God who uses his power in the service of love. What we have called "power-against" is the status quo of our world. In this paradigm, power is either an end-in-itself or else a means for selfish ends. Power in our world involves the ability to get a leg-up over everyone who stands in our way so that we can achieve our desires, or simply enjoy the pride of our victories. Power of this sort is the boast of every human kingdom and empire. It is a power which sometimes wears a benevolent mask, but in the end is obsessed with the superiority of "me," or of "us," over "them."

When we follow Jesus along the path which he laid down for us according to the Gospels, we see the great inversion of this paradigm of "power-against." Jesus turned humanistic notions of power on their head, although he was not so much turning them upside-down as much as returning them to right-side-up. Jesus lived out the power of God which is visible in the very act of creation: power exercised as a benevolent (even self-sacrificial) gift. Of course, Jesus did not reject the use of power. One of the first things said about Jesus in his ministry was that here was one whose teaching came with power (Mark 1:27). Obviously, his miracles were works of astonishing power. We have already considered how his resurrection is the very paradigm of the world-creating power of God. But Jesus's use of power was never about pride-of-place or pushing-around. Jesus rebuked his disciples over this very issue. We are told that instead of the rank-and-status games which they expected, "The Son of Man came not be served, but to serve, and to give his life as a ransom for many" (Mark 10:45). True power and greatness, according to God the Father and his son Jesus Christ, is about self-sacrificial love and servitude.

Christians like to talk about ideas such as servant-leadership, but one can get the sense that this is often mere lip-service. What would it look like for the church truly to view power—and to use it—the way Jesus taught and modeled for us? What would this look like in our various roles in our homes and workplaces, in schools, church elder boards, and political activities? What if in all these habitats for our vocations we consistently viewed our power as an opportunity to love, bless, serve, and lift up other people, rather than to lift ourselves up, win our personal or ideological battles, and in general try to get our own way?

There's a second, and perhaps related, lesson about the Christian life in God's plan to redeem power. This has to do with our relationship to the "realms, authorities, powers, and dominions." As we have already noted, these powers at work in the world's kingdoms and empires tend to operate according to the paradigm of "power-against" rather than "power-for." Jesus also stands over-against these powers-that-be. Here we observe what appears as a paradox: precisely in his commitment to creative, life-giving "power-for," God uses "power-against" the ones who live by the paradigm of "power-against." Perhaps we can say this more simply: God is the creator not the destroyer, yet because of this, he will destroy the destroyer. Or to say it altogether differently: God is love, but his love is not soft. Or with apologies to Bonhoeffer: God is gracious, but his grace is not cheap. This is not a defect of God's love and grace, but their perfection. Without God's holiness his grace would not be gracious, and without his power, his love would not be loving.

All of this is simply to say that in spite of the victory won at the cross, the world is still a battlefield of power-gone-wrong, and God is still fighting that battle. And, those who are his people have been conscripted into his army, forged by his grace into a weapon of courageous and self-sacrificial love. What this means in practice is that Christians are those who perpetrate the scandal of saying "Jesus alone is Lord" in a world which demands that we join in the chant that "We have no king but Caesar." It means that we stand with Shadrach, Meshach, and Abednego while the rest of the world is bowing before golden statues, even if it means being thrown into the furnace of the world's scorn. It means that we insist on saying "Jesus first" when there is pressure around us to say "America first" (or any other nation). We recognize no power but the world-creating power of God's love, no greatness but the greatness of God's glorious humility upon the cross, and no king but the king who died for his enemies.

Yet, I do not think this ordinarily means taking to the streets to publicly gnash our teeth at the government or other powers in the world. It means the courage of quietly serving and loving our neighbors in the name of Jesus, even while others are gnashing their teeth. We wage war, but not as the world does. We wield the power of God as he taught us to wield it: with self-sacrificial love. We resist the logic of power-against and embrace the logic of power-for. Of course, this in itself puts us against various ideologies of the world. We stand against the ideologies of prideful nationalism, but no less against the ideologies of quasi-benevolent bureaucracies. We stand against all ideologies which seek to use power for their own agendas and against their opponents, and we are called to use such power as we have to lovingly but uncompromisingly stand up for the good of our neighbors, especially those neighbors who are powerless to stand up for themselves—such as the poor, the alien, the widow, the orphan, and the unborn.

Many of these specific applications no doubt delve into highly disputed areas of controversy, but the bottom line is that to be a Christian involves unwavering loyalty to Jesus as Lord over all. This demands careful and critical attention to our various temptations toward idolatry, which might be obvious or subtle. The realms, authorities, powers, and dominions which demand our allegiance and our worship take many shapes and forms: fashionable consumerism, the comfortable pleasures which our world tells us we deserve, right-wing nationalism, left-wing moralistic utopianism—these and so many more comprise a pantheon of deities calling us to their temples to worship. The temple may be a shopping mall, a football stadium, a campaign rally, or even (we shudder) our own church. But among these, God has no temple but that living building which is the body of Christ: *his* church. We who are in Christ exist together as a testament to (and a manifestation of) the ultimate power and authority of the living God, and therefore a scandalous denial of the ultimacy of any worldly power. In the meantime—until the almighty power of God is consummated and his kingdom is finally fully enacted on earth—we live humbly in the mission for which God created us in his image, using the power which he has so humbly and scandalously delegated to us to bless the world through all our vocations and daily tasks.

Heavenly Father, we thank you again for being who you are, and so we thank you for being powerful—and not just powerful, but the very source of all power and might and strength. We thank you that your love is backed up by almighty power, and we praise your power for being grounded in self-sacrificial love. Lord, thank you for choosing to share your power with us. We are so unworthy of that gift with which you have entrusted us. It is a burden too heavy for us to bear on our own. And yet we know that we are not on our own. Thank you so much that through your Spirit and because of your Son Jesus Christ, your power—not ours but yours—is at work in us. So we look to you, Lord. While the world rages in its all its dysfunctional and tyrannical power, we look to you, knowing that your Christ, whom the world crucified, has been raised and now rules over all. It is to you, almighty God—Father, Son, and Holy Spirit—that we give our thanks and our praise and our adoration. Forgive us our idolatries and turn our hearts again to you. Crucify our idols on your cross and raise us again to live for you, knowing that we are yours and that your power is at work in us and among us and for us, for the glory of your great name. Amen.

3

The Scandal of Grace

Paraphrase: Ephesians 2:1–10

REMEMBER THAT YOU (MEMBERS of God's church) were dead through your trespasses and sins. You used to live in this death along with the rest of the world, which is under the power of this present realm. This power is the spirit who even now is at work among those who are still in rebellion against God. We were all once part of that company, living in the passionate lusts of the flesh. We were, like everyone else, children of wrath by nature. But God, who is rich in mercy, brought us into the life of Christ. He did this out of the great love which he had for us even while we were in death because of our rebellion against him. We were saved by his grace! Not only did he bring us into the life of Christ, he also raised us with him so that we would join him in the heavenly realms. He did this so that in the age to come, he would put on display his gracious kindness to us, which he gave us in Christ Jesus. You see, it is by grace you have been saved, through faith. None of this was your own doing, but is God's gift. None of us can boast as though it were the result of our work. For we are God's work, and are created in Christ Jesus to do the work which he has pre-purposed for us.

In the previous passage, Paul celebrated with his audience the fact of their membership in that glorious "we" which is held together by the power of God in Christ; a power which stands over and against all false powers of earth—and everywhere else. The power of God stands (already but not yet) triumphant against all these powers, and those who are in Christ live in that power.

It is tempting to let such intoxicatingly glorious truths go to our heads, and Ephesians 2 comes to the rescue on this point. We have not always been members of the "we" constituted by Christ and therefore the holy power of God. Nor is our membership in this solidarity—which we may, of course, simply call the church—an accomplishment for which we can take any credit. It is attributable only to the scandal of grace: the scandal whereby God rudely overturns all sensibilities of who-deserves-what and brings the beggars into the feast.

This passage finds its continuity with the previous passage in verse 2, where again Paul takes up the subject of "the powers." The powers over which Christ triumphed in his resurrection, that army arrayed against God, was a group which once held us captive; and in fact, all humanity is held captive by it apart from gracious intervention by God. But unfortunately, "held captive" doesn't put it strongly enough. We have not merely been prisoners but also soldiers in that army. Sin is a crime of which we are all both victims and perpetrators. We cannot really understand the truth which Paul has already expounded—that we belong to the power of God—without seeing it against the backdrop of our common human condition, in which we belong to the power of the enemy.

The Problem with Our World: Death

Everyone knows, both intuitively and experientially, that there is something wrong with the world and that human life is not as it should be. The reality of pain is a sobering reminder of this, as is the problem of death, that dark specter which floats over all human life. Death threatens to undo all our greatest accomplishments, to taint all that we find meaningful, and to separate us from our loved ones. It is difficult to overstate the extent to which human behavior and thought is motivated by a desire to find lasting meaning and happiness in the face of death. And why is it not only the case that we all must die, but that death visits the young and the innocent, and is frequently accompanied by horrible pain? Why is our world like this? In spite of all that is good in the world, why is there so much pain and suffering and death? What is wrong with the world that it should be this way?

Paul's answer is not one we like to hear: we are the problem. Death isn't so much something which happens to us as something which is a part of us, or a reality in which we live. Our very existence is naturally a kind of death. In Paul's words, we are dead in our trespasses and sins. This is true partly in the sense of future destiny: we all die, and even the liveliest person already has, in this sense, one foot in the grave. We are dead in our sins because death is the destiny for all sinful flesh. This brings us to the spiritual aspect of death, which is nothing else but the ultimate exile or separation: firstly from the world and from loved ones, but in the final scheme of things, from God himself. To sin is to separate oneself from the giver of life; therefore to be a sinner means, sooner or later, to die. In other words, we might say that death is the physical outworking of the spiritual disease called sin. To be dead in our sins means both a future destiny apart from God (a destiny in which sinful humans already partially participate), and also cooperation with God's cosmic enemies who together constitute the power of death: the world, the flesh, and the devil. It means being "on the wrong side of the tracks" regarding God; to be participants in the great rebellion against God and subject to the consequences of his justice. It means that we have revolted against the purpose for our lives in which God created us.

That is why death is connected to wrath. Paul describes the natural state of himself and his audience with the phrase "children of wrath." Most commenters and translators take this to mean *objects of God's wrath*. But could it be that Paul means quite literally that we are children of wrath: people conceived in a world which is a furnace of hatred against God and one another? Could he mean that the fire of wrath which will destroy us is one we ourselves have ignited in our enmity against God? Or perhaps Paul simply means the wrath against us which is characteristic of what we are as sinners—although he never does specify that the wrath belongs to God and not to us. But in any case, the reality is that we are placed under God's judgement; the same judgement which he has proclaimed against the powers and principalities of the world with which we are complicit. Our wrath against God, against his good purposes in the world, and against each other, is a blazing furnace which turns out to be the cause (and possibly even the instrument) of our own destruction. (For God's anger against the world does not arise on account of his wrath in itself, as though that were part of his essential nature, but this wrath is simply the outworking of his perfect goodness in response to the world's evil.) Our lives, like arrows shot from a bow, follow this trajectory of destructive judgement unless they are deflected by a force from the outside. The destiny is death: the finalization of the exile from God in which we already naturally live.

This is Paul's scandalous answer to the question, "What's wrong with the world?" The answer is: we are. The problem of death (which is perhaps the crux of our suffering) is at heart a problem of exile from God. Our problem in life is that we are on the wrong side of a cosmic war. There is an enemy: the great power of evil, suffering, and death, and we are naturally (whatever we would rather believe) coconspirators with that power.

The Solution: Life Given through Grace

The solution to the problem is just as scandalous. Humans are adept at pursuing solutions to their problems. It's one of the great things about our species. We're not content to sit passively in our mess. We've been endowed with big brains, and we like to put them to work. We come up with clever inventions of all sorts which make life easier and more comfortable, and seek out all kinds of ways to improve ourselves and our societies. So it's only intuitive for us when presented with a problem of this magnitude—that we're on the wrong side of a cosmic war against the creator—to roll up our sleeves and get to work with renewed energy. We've just got to work harder at being the kind of people of whom God approves. If the problem is human sin, then solution, it would seem, is human righteousness.

Unfortunately, our righteousness is actually part of the problem. It turns out that the problem of evil and suffering in the world, with which we are complicit, isn't of the sort which can be solved by our creative ingenuity or even our efforts of moral self-improvement. The problem is alienation in our relationship with our creator, and it is partly perpetuated by the belief that we can solve the problem on our own terms. Such human "solutions" promise to make us managers and powerbrokers in our relationship with God, and that itself is at the heart of what's wrong. Any real solution must come from God's side in the form of gracious forgiveness and reconciliation. Or to put it differently, the solution to human unrighteousness is not our righteousness, but rather God's righteousness, in which he includes us by his grace.

As it turns out, the one who condemns our evil is the very one who acts to save us from it. Out of the sinister web of sin, death, wrath, and judgement in whose grip the world is held, God brings us into the heavenly realm of life and love which, although painfully absent in the current order of things, is already a reality in Jesus Christ and is therefore present wherever there are people whose lives are enfolded into his own through faith and the power of the Holy Spirit.

Paul has once again contrasted the wicked powers of the world with God's loving power in Christ, and now we can see all the more clearly what role we play in the exercise of that power. As we have already seen, we who are in Christ are participants in and beneficiaries of the power of God over against the powers of evil, but now with the knowledge that we were once part of the latter. God's work of transformation from death to life is not merely a work of regenerating individual depraved souls, but of inducting captive enemies into God's camp. Through faith we have entered a new realm. Out of the realm of death, we have entered life. God brings rebel soldiers who repent into his own country as citizens. Enemies of God become children of God. As we will see in the next passage, strangers and foreigners are brought so close to God that they become his temple.

So, although we have all been part of the problem, God in his grace makes us part of the solution. Our problem is an alienated existence: both from God personally, and from the life in which we live out the purposes he has destined for us. In the beginning, God predestined us to "be holy and blameless before him" (1:4). Ephesians 2:1–3 shows how the human race (including each one of us) has deviated from this destiny. Verses 4–10 describe how God has pulled his people back into it. God's gracious love gives us life; that is, fellowship with God where previously there was enmity. It also highlights the cosmic purposes at work in God's redeeming grace: to put his loving kindness on display in us for all eternity. This reminds us of all that Paul wrote in chapter 1 about our redemption being "for the praise of his glorious grace." Creation and redemption alike draw us, by sheer grace, to center of the drama of reality. And here in this passage we are again reminded that God has cast us in a role in this drama. "For we are God's work, and are created in Christ Jesus to do the work which he has pre-purposed for us."

This is a glorious truth no less intoxicating. But unlike the strong liquor of human pride, which is distilled from non-reality, the wine of our communion with Christ flows from the truth: that we are unworthy but beloved sinners, redeemed by (and for) the work of God. Our lives are grounded in the truth of God's grace; a truth which lies like a bedrock beneath the shifting sand of our sin.

The Scandal of Grace

For those who have been Christians for any significant length of time, there is a serious risk that the sharp edge of the message of grace has been worn dull for us through over-familiarity. We need to be reminded of the scandal of grace. Why should such good news be scandalous? There are at least two reasons.

First, grace scandalizes our sense of justice; our intuition about who-deserves-what. Ephesians 2 celebrates grace in a manner grateful of our status as recipients. But there are other passages of Scripture which highlight its scandalous nature.

For example, the book of Jonah tells the story of a prophet who was scandalized by God's grace for the unworthy. Jonah flees to Tarshish because he wants no part in a mission of mercy for the Ninevites, those wicked enemies of Israel. Jonah's dispute with God over this is surprisingly direct. He tells God, after the Ninevites have repented, "This is what I tried to forestall by fleeing to Tarshish. I knew that you are a gracious and compassionate God, slow to anger and abounding in love, a God who relents in sending calamity" (Jonah 4:2). The obvious irony here is that these are words normally regarded as high praise and thanksgiving, as we see in Psalm 103:8. Yet here they are the brunt of Jonah's criticism. Grace is beautiful to us when it is given to those we think are deserving, but it smacks of unfairness when granted to people who we think need to be punished. But such an intuition is nothing other than evidence that we really don't understand grace, which by its very nature is a gift to the undeserving. That leads us to another great irony in the story of Jonah. The prophet laments the fact that Israel's enemies, whom he regards as so undeserving of mercy, have received it from God. He himself throughout the story shows every kind of hardness of heart we can imagine, from blatant disobedience to God's command, to a peevish entitlement regarding a simple shade-giving plant, sins for which God shows surprising patience. Yet he has the gall to complain of God's mercy for the undeserving!

We meet a similar kind of person in Jesus's parable of the prodigal son: the older son who resents the lavish forgiveness the father has poured out on his wayward younger brother when he returns. Whereas the younger brother has been absurdly disrespectful to the father through his demand to receive the inheritance early and has lived foolishly and wickedly in the extreme, the older brother is the very picture of filial piety. His life all along has been one of dutiful obedience. In that respect he strikes us as a better figure than Jonah. But in his failure to grasp the counter-intuitive logic of mercy, he is just like the runaway prophet. To both, grace given to those they deem undeserving is both a mystery and an outrage.

We would be quite wrong to examine either of these biblical figures without perceiving that we are looking in a mirror. When we believe that we are in the right, we are sticklers about justice and scandalized by grace. We want those who have hurt us—or perhaps anyone we deem to have fallen short of our own righteous standards—to get their comeuppance. Of course, when we have been made aware of our own grievous wrongdoings, we change our tune. We are happy for exceptions to justice when they are in our favor.

But all this shows how very unlike God we are. God too is a stickler about justice—in fact, more so than any of us. And yet somehow, at the same time, he is more gracious than we can comprehend. Is this a great theological contradiction? Almost. It is rather a paradox of divine perfection which has been reconciled on the cross of Jesus Christ. The cross is the place of collision between God's justice against sin and his gracious mercy for sinners. God in Christ took the just wrath for which we were destined upon himself and embraced us in a most costly forgiveness.

How do we respond to this scandalous inversion of who-deserves-what, especially when we realize that it is in our favor? That's where we perceive a second scandal of grace: the outrage against our pride which is incurred when we realize that any favorable relation to God is due to his mercy, not our merit. After all, we don't merely want good things for ourselves; we also want the satisfaction of feeling that we deserve them. And grace denies us such satisfaction.

Jesus famously said that just as the sick, not the healthy, are those who need doctors, he came to save not the righteous, but sinners (Matt 9:11–13). The acceptance of grace requires us to acknowledge the bitter truth that we can't do it on our own. This shouldn't be a hard pill for us to swallow, for it is quite simply the truth. But pride has a way of blocking the truth from view. That might actually be close to the heart of what pride is: a condition of being out-of-touch with the truth, in which we are mistaken about the facts of who we are, of who God is, and the real relation between those facts. It's part of the spiritual disease for which grace is the cure. And while the bad news is that pride tends to deny the need for the grace that is so needed, the good news is that grace, once received, gouges out our pride like a surgeon's scalpel. Of course that is a painful process, but healing very often is. The fact that grace scandalizes and offends our sense of pride is often a deterrent from receiving it, but this scandal is also part of the very mechanism whereby grace does its healing work. We desperately need to be torn away from the lie that "I'm okay, you're okay" and receive the truth that that we are in fact enemies of God, and that apart from his grace, we can't be anything else. There are certain points in our self-centered lives at which we all need some therapeutic humiliation.

But despite the fact that grace is humiliating to our pride, that is not its final result. The outcome of grace depicted in Ephesians 2 is not God gloating over the pitiful objects of his condescension, but rather God lifting these pitiful creatures into the heavenly realm, where they receive the honor of displaying God's mercy for all eternity. This is a double-edged truth. On the one hand, our eternal office is one which serves as a humbling reminder of what we were: unworthy sinners. On the other, it is an office served by dwelling within the very cloud of God's glory. By being restored to our creation-calling to display God's glorious image, we are made to be partakers and beneficiaries in that glory. And the fact that we were once utter enemies of God makes his glory shine off us all the brighter.

Ephesians 2:10 presents another way of looking at the same truth regarding the result of God's grace: we become not shameful beggars, but God's workmanship (the text even justifies us using the word "masterpiece").[1] We are a restored work of God, and not in the passive sense of a reconditioned antique which has been polished to sit on a shelf, but rather the kind of work which itself has work to do. We are restored to the vocations which God intended for us from the very beginning: to be a holy and blameless people who put his goodness, wisdom, and love on display.

Myths about Grace

At this point, we are equipped to confront head-on certain popular myths about grace. After all, because grace is scandalous, it is frequently misunderstood. However, as we will see, some of the wrong thinking which crops up around the concept of grace comes from the opposite direction we have considered. We see this in the first myth we will examine.

---

1. See, for example, the New Living Translation of Ephesians 2:10.

Myth 1: Grace is Tolerance of Sin

As self-righteous persons, we tend to be outraged by grace. But at the same time, as sinful persons, we want such grace as we get to be cheap. We want it to make us feel good, and to come with no strings attached. Perhaps we see this especially in modern presuppositions about God's love. It is almost axiomatic for people now to believe that God is love, although perhaps without usually thinking very deeply about what this really means. What it too often means for us is merely this: that God doesn't really have any serious problems with us or what we do. Oh yes, God wants us to behave ourselves. But when it comes down to it, he's a gentle soul who would never really want to seriously punish anyone. This view of God's love and grace at bottom is really identical with the postmodern creed that "I'm okay, you're okay."

Can we see the shift that has taken place here? Grace, as such, is no longer a statement about God or the surprising act of costly forgiveness he has undertaken. It's really more a statement about ourselves; namely that God couldn't possibly have any really serious problem with us, the reason being that while we might have some rough edges, we are at bottom more or less decent people. Of course God wouldn't really be mad at us! What we mean by God's grace, in this condition, involves two assumptions: first, that there's nothing seriously wrong with us, and second, that when we do slip up, God is happy to let it slide. Grace is viewed as mere tolerance for sin, and this view is sustained by a high view of our own righteousness.

While this view of grace (what Dietrich Bonhoeffer called cheap grace) might look like the opposite of the kind of self-righteousness we examined above, I think it's really quite closely related. Cheap grace is respectable grace. Receiving it doesn't require any admission of the real dire straits we are in. It is not the grace which the person who knows he is wicked (like the thief on the cross) cries out for on his death bed. This watered-down grace is merely a comfort to assuage the little guilts of those people who don't think they have much to feel guilty about in the first place. We like to think that we are mostly good people, and whenever we do make a little mistake—well, there's always grace for that.

Not only does such a view of grace underestimate our own sin, it also fundamentally misunderstands God's strategy of redemption. Cheap grace is actually non-grace. Instead of celebrating God's forgiveness, we imply that God actually doesn't have all that much to forgive. But God has much to forgive. We have not, after all, merely been naughty children. We have been enemies of God, participants in the war which the powers of evil are waging against his kingdom. And God, who is infinitely good, never for a moment gave us a free pass with a little wink. The evil in which we have all been complicit demands one of two things: our own destruction, or else God taking the destruction into himself, such as he accomplished in Christ on the cross. God doesn't tolerate sin. He forgives it only at infinitely great cost to himself. Our problem, then, is not that we make too much of God's love, but too little. Only when we appreciate the depth of our sin and extent of God's holiness, can we come anywhere near comprehending what his love actually means.

Perhaps there's a lesson here for our own approach to sin and evil in the world. Our modern sensibilities say a lot about tolerance, but very little about genuine love. Tolerance, of course, is very important when it comes to extending hospitality, kindness, and respect to people who are different from us in terms of beliefs and backgrounds. But it is no substitute for genuine love. Love, of the sort which comes from God, never tolerates evil. It responds to evil with an astonishing combination of utter opposition and self-sacrificial forgiveness. To learn to love this way, we have the work of a lifetime (and probably then some) cut out for us.

Myth 2: Grace is an End-In-Itself

The above view of grace—that it is mere tolerance—is critiqued for being too soft. Here is another view of grace which is also too soft, although in a different way. It is the notion that God has been gracious to us for no other reason than that we should enjoy the benefits of a privileged status. At bottom, this is a very self-centered view of grace: it's all about me and the good things I get out of the arrangement.

Despite the ultimate self-centeredness of this idea, I think it often arises out of some important truths and good instincts. We are perhaps rightly cautious about dwelling on *reasons* for divine grace, because they might seem to undermine it as a sheer, underserved gift. Certainly we want to avoid the idea that God has been gracious to us because of any good thing we have done. We also want to avoid an overly utilitarian view of grace, in which we are nothing more than a cog in God's cosmic plan, and that our salvation has little to do with a particular loving affection for us. We rightly cherish the fact that God's grace emerges out the mystery of his sheer gratuitous love for underserving people.

But we don't do justice to this text and others like it when we think that God has saved people just so that they can, well, *be saved*. We are saved *for* something. Perhaps we are cogs in God's plan after all, although that may be an ugly way of putting it. We must be humble enough to recognize our own insignificance in comparison to the vastness of our universe, let alone to the God who created it. If we begin with an appropriately God-centered humility, being involved even as a "cog" in his redemptive work is an almost outrageous honor. And, moreover, "cog" is simply not the right word. The universe is not a machine, and neither are we. Redemption seems to be an intensely personal enterprise, and it is as redeemed-and-redeeming *persons* that God is interested in us.

The bad news about grace is that it doesn't leave us sitting at ease without anything more to do. But this bad news is actually good news. Do we really want an existence like that? We were created to till the garden of God; to play a part in his great drama; to be personally and actively involved in his wonderful works. We have been saved *from* an existence of separation from God; we are saved *to* an existence of union with him by participating in his ongoing work of redemption. We should not for a moment think that this threatens our conviction that grace is a free gift. It is not at all as though God gives us a job so that we can try to pay him back for all he has done for us. Participation in his glorious work is in fact part of the gift.

If we are well acquainted with the biblical story of redemption, none of this should surprise us. We think back to the commissioning of Abraham in Genesis 12, in which God not only promised that Abraham and his offspring would be blessed, but that all peoples would be blessed through them. They were never meant merely to be recipients of God's blessing, but to function like a reflective surface radiating those blessings out to all nations. We shouldn't think of Israel's status as a recipient of blessing and their vocation to bless the nation as two entirely separate things. Perhaps part of the blessing itself was the honor of being involved with its propagation in the world.

So too with the people whom Paul describes as "blessed in the heavenly realms with every spiritual blessing in Christ" (1:3). Here in 2:6 we read about the same thing in more detail: that we have in fact been lifted into that heavenly realm in union with Jesus Christ, and that here we enjoy the supreme blessing of being a means by which God's glorious grace is praised for all eternity. This is the paradox of true happiness: it is not found merely in the attainment of great things for ourselves, but in our joyful participation in great realities beyond ourselves.²

In short, God's grace for us is not an end-in-itself or a gift given merely for our enjoyment of a glorified status. It is something less "us-centered" and therefore much better: the privilege of eternal involvement in the glory of God.

Myth 3: Grace and works are opposed to one another

Myths 2 and 3 are closely connected. Myth 2 is that grace is merely something good for us to enjoy without involving us in the further work of redemption and God's glory, and one of the reasons why it's easy to believe this myth is that many of us have been taught to see the terms *grace* and *works* in diametrically opposed categories. Again, there are some good reasons for this, not least of which is the strong statement in Ephesians 2:8, "For grace you have been saved, not by works." That we are reconciled to God through his gracious initiative and not through any merit or deservingness of our own is central to the Christian gospel. This is what is meant by the opposition to what is sometimes called "works salvation," or else "legalism," or with an eye to ancient church history, "Pelagianism." This insistence that salvation is not an achievement of human moral effort is found perhaps most dramatically in the protestant reformers, especially Martin Luther. And this has all been for good reason. As we have already observed, it's in our human nature to want to take credit for what we do and to keep up the illusion that God is in our pocket through our own laborious piety.

The problem comes in when we learn to shudder at all talk about morality and good works as "legalism." According to this understanding, grace has abolished all sense of human responsibility. God has forgiven us free and clear, so why should we bother about all that?

---

2. For those who are interested in philosophy, there's a connection here with the philosophical/theological tradition called the *beatific vision* which was taught, in various versions, by Augustine and Thomas Aquinas, with some theoretical influence from Plato and Aristotle. The *beatific vision* is a way of framing the meaning and teleology (final goal) of human life as the supreme happiness (*eudemonia*) of gazing upon and enjoying that which is most intrinsically and infinitely good. The *beatific vision* which we find in Scripture is, if we may dare to say so, even better than this perhaps somewhat passive picture of eternal admiration. The Christian view of eternal blessedness is one in which we are privileged not only to admire God's glory, but in addition, to relationally participate in it through membership in the worshipping community of his redeemed image-bearers.

Of course, those who say so have a point. It is a real danger that the logic of merit will creep back into our relationship with God, in which case we begin to think that our behavior, for good or ill, is what determines God's love and acceptance of us.

Which way is it? Is grace a gift with no strings attached which puts us at liberty to live however we like, or is grace just in fact another law which holds us under a behavioral obligation?

We could well say that those are opposite errors, and perhaps equally dangerous. Both pull us away from the new relation to God which is the true outcome of grace. Both roads, while seeming to head off in opposite directions, are plotted with the same purpose of avoiding God himself.

Timothy Keller has described this very well in his reading of the parable of the Prodigal Son (or as he likes to call it, the Two Lost Sons).[3] As we have already seen, the older brother in the story resents the scandalous unfairness he sees in his father's lavish grace for the younger son. But Keller points out that both sons, through opposite lifestyles, live by the same ultimate principle: they both care more about getting their father's things than they care about their relationship with the father himself. The younger son is rude and direct. He demands his inheritance up front and runs off with it to live in overt rebellion. The older son is much better behaved, but his good behavior is, in the long run, a calculated attempt to earn a good standing. He sees his years of service for his father not as a work of loving gratitude for life in his father's household, but as a slavish toil which ought to have merited him the honor which has been freely (and in his eyes, unjustly) thrown upon the returned prodigal.

We see here where both legalism and licentiousness go astray, by different paths, to the same end. Grace is the reality that God has freely given us the gift of himself. He has welcomed us all back to his side. But neither legalism nor license are really interested in that. They want to either use God, or avoid him altogether, for our own self-centered purposes.

So what is grace, then?

We could expend many words in probing out the psychology of rebellion against God and how it manifests itself in various misunderstandings of his grace. But our time now is better spent thinking about what God's grace really is. To make a long story short, God's grace is neither permission to sin nor law under a new name. It is a welcome into a reconciled relationship with God, earned for us by his own costly sacrifice in Christ,

---

3. Keller, *Prodigal God*, 20–54.

which sets us free to become that which he created us to be. Grace is a freedom, but not freedom to turn back to the slave-master of sin, for that would be no freedom at all. It is a freedom from the punishment sin brings, and ultimately too from sin's mastery. But it is not just a *freedom-from*. It is, perhaps even more importantly, a *freedom-to*.

We might picture it this way. A convict sits in his prison cell for a crime he has committed. Someone comes along and pays his debt for him. The warden opens the cell door, and he is free to leave the cell. Suppose the prisoner chooses to stay. "After all," he says, "I'm a free man. Nobody can make me leave." This is what a person is like who sees the grace of God merely as an opportunity to keep living as-is without the guilt. Yes, he is free, but he doesn't grasp the point of his freedom. God has paid our debt so that we can leave the prison which is the old realm of sin and death. He has granted us entrance into the new realm of life in Christ. Of course, old habits die hard, it takes a lifetime (and then some) to learn to live like a member of this new realm, and we enjoy wonderful assurance of God's ongoing patience and forgiveness in the meantime. But a member of this new realm is what we are in Christ, and if we have no interest in that new life, it seems we haven't really understood what God's grace is about in the first place. God has redeemed us from the dark prison of sin and brought us out into the bright day of his glory, in which we can run free to do the glorious tasks he created us to enjoy. Why would we want to shrink back from this so as to keep living according to the norms of the world? Perhaps because we have seen grace merely as a clever trick for getting us off the hook, rather than an invitation into life itself.[4]

Now we can see most clearly the sense of verses 8–10: "It is by grace you have been saved, through faith. None of this was your own doing, but is God's gift. None of us can boast as though it were the result our work. For we are God's work, and are created in Christ Jesus to do the work which he has pre-purposed for us." We are not saved by works, but we are in fact

---

4. Perhaps it is helpful here to regard earthly sin and eternal punishment not as two separate things related to each other as cause and effect, but rather simply the same thing in different stages of development. It's not so much the case that we sin, and then as a secondary consequence of that, we receive the punishment of death and hell. Sin, as rebellion against the source of all goodness and life, *is* death and hell, in its embryonic form. Similarly, heaven is not so much a reward in which we receive eternal life with God because of good behavior—whether ours or Christ's. Heaven *is* in fact the reconciled life with God which believers enjoy now through Christ in an embryonic form. Eternity is the great birdcage in which all temporal eggs will hatch and become more obviously that which they already are. (Said with a nod to Lewis, *Mere Christianity*, 169.)

saved *for* works, rightly understood. Not mere moral behavior (although that is a part of it), but the work which God has always meant to accomplish in and through us. Salvation is not our own work, for we ourselves are God's work, a work in which he means for us to cooperate with him now and into eternity.

We also shouldn't miss the connection between 2:10 and 1:4, which says that God chose us in Christ before the foundation of the world to be holy and blameless in his sight. Maybe we would like for Paul to have been clearer by adding the word "saved" to "holy and blameless," but I suspect that he would have regarded that as a redundancy. To be saved is to be restored to the great purposes for which God created us. It is to be enfolded into the destiny which he intended for all humanity and which has been realized in Jesus Christ. This destiny, for which we have been created and now recreated, is the vocation of glorifying God as his holy image-bearers, purified and blameless on account of his work in us.

Conclusion

What does it mean really to grasp this as God's people? Perhaps we now see why, in the previous passage, Paul emphasized *knowledge* in his prayers for the Ephesians. Coming to a proper understanding of who and what we are in Christ, and what this means for our everyday lives, is surely a monumental task. The rest of Ephesians will help us in that task, but this passage (2:1–10) leaves us with its own particular questions to ponder.

For instance, what is grace? That is a simple question but a terribly important one. Ephesians 2 depicts grace as much more than a particular event in time in which we received salvation, but an ongoing activity of God, in and through us, which makes fuller sense of our salvation. We are brought up against what perhaps feels like a paradox here: that God's grace is a matter of our absolute dependency, yet never of our passivity. Grace doesn't merely pull us into a privileged status. It draws us into the work of God, in which he means to manifest his glory. Perhaps we would say it better this way: grace pulls us into a privileged status precisely *by* drawing us into his glorious work.

A teacher of mine once emphasized the importance of learning the personal skill he called "resting in the saddle." That seems to encompass the tension we find in the implications of grace. It gives us perfect rest. At the same time, it gives us a job to do. But those are not, in fact, two different things.

Do our churches know how to "rest in the saddle?" We have complacent churches who are content with the status quo, full of people who, having been saved, are content to ride their salvation like a lazy river and watch the world go by. But grace is not merely salvation according to our often watered-down definition of that word. To receive God's grace and his salvation is to be made truly alive. Everyone (for now) has a heartbeat, but what does it mean to be truly alive? If we take Ephesians seriously, it involves being pulled out of the status quo of the world and into realm of God—and therefore also the work of God. Many of our churches need to think through what it means to get in the saddle of God's grace. There is a whole world around us which is starving for it, and we, the church, are God's workmanship—his hand-carved instrument—for reaching out to this world.

But then, there are many churches which know nothing but frenetic activity. Their pulpit might be a tower of salvation-by-grace-alone, but their boardroom is a frenzied workshop of practical Pelagianism. It is never said out loud, nor even probably thought consciously, but often our way of conducting the life of the church is laden with the assumption that we have something to earn and prove for ourselves. We feel it is up to us to build the church. But the church is not, and never was, an achievement built by our work. The church is simply a people abiding in the greatness of God and his work for us; in the truth that "On this rock I will build my church, and the gates of hell will not prevail against it." But of course, his work is still unfolding in and through us. The church in which this truth is grasped may in fact be just as busy as the church which is trying to prove itself, but there is an underlying difference which manifests in the quality of their activities. They are not working compulsively toward a place of strength, but *from* it, propelled on, as it were, by the explosive power of the gospel. Their work is permeated by the sense of confidence and joy characteristic of those who are motivated by gratitude and the assurance that their work, having already been actually accomplished by Christ, cannot at this point fail. The church was meant to put God's grace and glory on display, not his anxiety.

Of course, the lessons which we apply corporately also need to be pondered individually. Ephesians 2 gives believers in Christ great assurance, but at the same time a sense of grateful responsibility. There is no work hanging over us to do, but God means to do much work in and through us, and involvement with it is a great privilege. We have the courage to face each day with its fresh challenges and inevitable failures knowing that there is no mistake we can make for which God in Christ has not already worked his forgiveness. And yet grace is by no means a tolerance of sin. The eventual goal of God's grace is nothing less than the transformation of sinners into a divine masterpiece. God is quite serious about that. His grace does not mean merely putting up with caterpillars; he insists on turning them into butterflies. Grace is not the suspension of God's opposition to evil, but quite the opposite. It is his ingenious military strategy in his war against evil, through which he takes the brunt of it on himself and draws the undeserving into his victory.

This is a victory whose full consequences we still await and anticipate, yet whose certain accomplishment we already enact in our daily work. This has the potential to reframe and to glorify every little thing we do. Are we prepared to see all the little tasks of our lives, as well as the big ones, as opportunities to function as the workmanship of God, for the praise of his glory? Are we willing, as unworthy but beloved recipients of God's grace, to live as though we are celebrating and reflecting this miracle that those around us may see and give praise to God? This is the willingness in which God means to work through us for the redemption of the world.

Lord, we are thankful that you are an infinitely good God. We give you thanks and praise for your holiness, in which you are not okay with the way things are in the world. We find assurance in your justice. And yet, we know that we too are part of the problem in the world. And for this we tremble, but for the knowledge of your great love and mercy. Thank you, Lord, for your grace and forgiveness, which you have extended to us at the cost of your very life, given to us through Jesus Christ on the cross. We marvel at this meeting of holiness and love. But it is more than a source of amazement for us; it is our very life. You have rescued us from the dominion of darkness and drawn us into the realm of light; the realm of your beloved and victorious son, Jesus Christ. Lord, we thank for loving us dearly even while we were in sin, and not only that, but also for loving us too much to leave us there. For this we are not only grateful, but also greatly humbled. Out of rebels like us you have made for yourself a work of art, a living testament to your love, and a tool for your ongoing work of redemption. Our prayer, Lord, is that having redeemed us at such a price and for such a purpose, you will teach us day by day to inhabit that purpose in union with your son, Jesus Christ. Mold us and shape us into your workmanship, and may your glory be seen in us, this very day and into eternity. To you be the honor and the glory in all the world, in the name of your son who reigns, and by the power of your Holy Spirit. Amen.

4

The Scandal of Unity

Paraphrase: Ephesians 2:11-22

So AGAIN, REMEMBER WHAT *you used to be. You who are Gentiles by birth, who are called "the uncircumcised" by those who call themselves "the circumcised" (regarding the physical circumcision made in the flesh by human hands), remember that when you were apart from Christ, you were aliens from God's people Israel and strangers from the covenant of promise. You were out there in the world, without God and without hope.*

But now, in Christ Jesus, you who were once far away (enemies and strangers) have been brought near by the blood of Christ. For he is our peace. In his flesh he has made both groups (Jews and Gentiles) into a single group. He's broken down the wall which divided them, destroying that old hostility. In him the law, with all the divisions imposed by its commandments and ordinances, has been abolished. He has done this in order that he might create in himself one new humanity in place of the two, so that peace might be made between them, and that they together might have peace with God. They are reconciled to God as one body; for together they are in the one body of Jesus on the cross, on which our hostility has been put to death. In this way Christ proclaimed peace for both those who were far away and for those who were near. Through Christ both groups have access in one Spirit to the Father. So then, you are no longer strangers and aliens, but citizens with all God's holy people, members together of his household, which is built on the foundation of the apostles and prophets, with Christ Jesus himself as the cornerstone. In him, this whole building of which we are members is joined together and rises to become the Lord's own holy temple. In him you are being built up together by the Spirit to be God's dwelling place.

We can see how Paul's argument in Ephesians is unfolding: the scandal of particularity (God's eternal purpose in Christ) is enacted through a scandalous use of power (delegating it to fallible beings) which is vindicated by the scandal of grace (bringing these fallen image-bearers back into the fold of his power and purpose). Now, in this passage, we begin to see the social implications of all this.

However, we shouldn't thereby assume that Paul has ventured into an altogether new topic. In many ways, this passage mimics the one which came before it. Both begin with a description of "what you were" and proceed to describe God's work of redemption from that condition. Both halves of Ephesians 2 describe the same problem and the same solution. But 2:11–22 describes them from some new vantage points; namely the history of God's people Israel and the new social solidarity which is created among God's people in Christ.

Human Life as a (Damaged) Relational Network

In the previous passage, we explored the problem of the human condition: the reign of sin and death, those cosmic powers which oppress humanity but with which we are complicit. Sin and death are really different words referring to the same reality, which can be more or less summed up in the word *exile*. Sin is a self-imposed exile from God through rebellion against him, and it results in death, which is the condition of being cut off from the life which is God's generous gift.

This present passage invites us to reflect on this even further; namely by seeing that exile from God also involves exile from one another and our human communities. This is a connection which takes us all the way back to the creation account in Genesis, which describes human life as embedded in a relational network. The primary human relation is with our creator, God above us, in whose image we are made and to whom we are ultimately responsible. This relation is lived out in the context of our creaturely relations: with our fellow humans beside us, with whom we have loving fellowship, and with the world beneath us, which is the arena of our vocation to represent the benevolent rule of God. All of these relations are clearly visible in Genesis 1–2. In Genesis 3, after Adam and Eve disobey

God, we can see the breakdown of all three relationships. The punishment is banishment from the garden and ultimately death; in short, exile from the presence of God. Part of the curse is a new sense of tension and estrangement between the husband and his wife, in which "her desire will be for her husband, and he shall rule over her." (We can note in passing that a relationship which was previously marked by loving "power-for" one another now is tainted with a sense of "power-against.") And also, the human vocational relationship to the earth itself is damaged, since the work of the farmer's hands will be difficult and laden with thorns. The situation, then, is a threefold exile. Alienation in our most essential relationship—between us and our creator—leads to brokenness in all other relationships. The reason for this is clearer when we realize that these three relationships (God, others, world) were never meant to be to separate from each other at all, but an integrated means whereby we live out and celebrate our relationship with God. All relations and activities in the world were meant to be habitats for receiving, enjoying, and reflecting back the love of God. Genesis 4–11 goes on to show the progressive breakdown of these relationships in the human community, and in fact, this sets the tone for the rest of the Old Testament, which is dominated by the theme of exile. Israel turns out to be a people who, while created to know God and make him known among the nations, continuously find themselves estranged from him, from each other, and from their own land. The problem of exile seems to hang over the whole Old Testament, and leaves us wondering "How, in light of the persistent problem of sin and brokenness, will God's people really come home and enjoy his presence? Will God somehow overcome the divisions which separate humanity from himself, from one another, and from the vocations he has purposed for them in the world?"

These are intensely biblical questions, and they are also universal ones. We all ask them, whether or not we use the scriptural vocabulary. Who are we, really? Why is our sense of purpose and belonging in the world so fragile? Why can't we really seem to be quite at home in the world, with others, or with ourselves for that matter? If there is a higher power or purpose behind our existence, why does it (or he) seem so far out of reach? These are all different ways of asking the same question: why are we "cut-off" or in exile? The Old Testament presents an answer to this: we have rebelled against our creator and are therefore estranged from him. But the question remains: can we really "come home?" And if so, how? Can God's purposes for his people win out in the face of the ongoing problem of sin? These are questions to which the New Testament, in a whole variety of ways, presents God's answer: Jesus Christ.

In its own way, Ephesians makes that clear. Through God's grace in Christ we are returned to his side in the land of the living; reconciled as his beloved children. Ephesians also affirms (although perhaps more indirectly) that in Christ our vocational relationship to the world is redeemed. For example, 2:10 celebrates how the grace of God restores us to the works which he has purposed for us. And this passage, 2:11–22, shows very clearly that our reconciliation with God is inseparable from restored relationships with one another.

Perhaps we can bring this closer to home. The problems of human alienation, division, and hostility are deeply integrated with the condition of death and evil. In fact, we might say that when we strip away the abstractions in words such "evil" and "suffering" and look at particular instances of these conditions, there is usually—perhaps almost always—a social or relational factor. This is obvious in cases like war and domestic violence. But it is also a factor even in matters such as personal illness. A person who is suffering cancer, even while they receive the love and compassion of family and friends and doctors, is in one sense completely alone with their suffering. People empathize, but nobody can truly enter their pain. This creates even more pain—not only for the person who suffers, but for the people who love them and wish that there was something they could do—they would even take the pain upon themselves if they could. Also, as we have already noted, all physical ailments are part of our basic condition of mortality, and death appears from our side to be utter separation from the human family. In short, because humans are social creatures, all their problems (whether by cause or effect) have social dimensions.

This is why God's solution has a social dimension, too. The entire scriptural story is one in which the wise and loving creator God seeks to restore the world he has made after things have gone so wrong because of the misuse of creaturely power in rebellion against him. The solution which we see God use throughout the story is not the sort we might expect of an all-powerful God. He doesn't just snap his fingers and recreate the world without the pain and evil. He does, in fact, recreate the world, and every Christian is a part of that act of recreation. But the problem, which involves rebellious wills rather than broken machinery, is an intensely personal one, and this requires a personal solution which lies outside the realm of strict cause-and-effect. God's solution is to create a people—not just renewed individuals, but a new *people*; a society of sons and daughters of God. We know that he ultimately did this through his own begotten son, Jesus Christ, whom he sent into the world so that we may be united with him and thereby drawn into his family. We also know that God's solution involved unimaginable self-sacrifice on his part. Sin and death are relational wounds and their healing requires sacrificial love, which God himself has poured out for us.[1]

God's Covenant with his People

We first see the beginning stage of God's "people-solution" in the people called Israel, the offspring of Abraham. God's election of Israel forms the backdrop to what Paul writes here in Ephesians 2 about the relationship between the circumcised and the uncircumcised. Circumcision, we remember, was given to Abraham and all his offspring as the sign of the covenant. *Covenant* may be more or less defined as a relationship between God and his people which is established on the basis of his unconditional gracious promise, but which entails faithfulness and obedience on the part of the people to fully benefit from that gracious promise. We could well say that covenant is one of the main themes of Scripture (both Old and New Testaments together), and that it is central to God's whole strategy of redemption. How it accomplishes this has already been described: the basic problem of the world is a people-problem, but God in his grace invites people to become part of his solution. God redeems people by calling them into life-changing relationships with him and each other which are founded on his gracious love and his promises for future glory. The great fulfillment of the covenant is Jesus Christ, who embodies both the faithfulness of God, and the human faithfulness which is the appropriate response to God's covenant. His death on the cross uniquely manifests the sacrificial

1. We see here a major problem with the problem of evil as it usually articulated, in which we wonder how there can be a good and almighty God who allows evil. This is problematic for us because we assume that evil/suffering is the sort of problem God could just solve with the snap of his fingers. Perhaps what the problem of evil, so formulated, shows, is that we don't really understand the problem, nor the solution which God has already initiated. The problem of evil is one which lives in the relational world of rebellion, pride, and hatred, not the cause-and-effect world which is usually the domain of modern approaches to problem-solving. It's a relational problem which involves a relational solution, which God has introduced in Jesus Christ, his cross, and the people remade in his image.

love and perfect justice of God in reconciling the relational wound of sin. Jesus Christ alone is the real embodiment of all that Israel (and in fact humankind) was meant to be, and we are invited to partake in the reality of his life, death, and resurrection as we enter union with him by faith. This is a relationship between God and his people, established by sheer grace in Jesus Christ, but entailing a new life for us, oriented around God's purposes for us in creation and redemption. It is a relationship which is entered only through faith, and is therefore open to people of all nations and ethnicities. That is the meaning of covenant in the Christian sense.

But like all earthshaking acts of God, this took time for God's people to understand. The idea that God's chosen people were merely the circumcised (the offspring of Abraham) was deeply ingrained in the minds of the first followers of Jesus, who of course were Jews. God had in fact been teaching his people (through both circumcision and the law) for thousands of years that they were unique and separate from all other nations of the world. For centuries they had believed (partly correctly) that the physical offspring of Abraham alone were God's people. It required a major paradigm shift for them to recognize the good news: that gentiles could now be grafted into God's people simply through faith in Jesus Christ. There are several factors which we need to consider in order to understand this.

First, as already indicated, the belief on the part of the Jews that they alone were children of the promise was only partly correct. It is true that God created a unique covenant with Abraham and his offspring. But a real relationship with the living God was never an automatic affair because of genetics. Personal faith was always the critical ingredient. Throughout the Old Testament, Israel sometimes seemed to "miss the boat" by their failure to trust the living God through their attractions to idols, national powers, or wealth attained by injustice. The prophets made it clear that for these reasons, many Israelites would miss out on the promises associated with membership in God's people, and would in fact come under his judgement. Further, we find examples of God-fearing gentiles even in the Old Testament who possessed a faith-relation to God which some Israelites missed. Rahab, Ruth, and Naaman come to mind. God's unique covenant with Israel was always a tool for building a people and reaching the world, never a limitation on the reach of God's redemption. A reconciled relationship to God has always, ultimately, been mediated by a response of faith to his gracious initiative, and never strictly by the physical facts of circumcision and Abrahamic descent.

Second and relatedly, Israel was prone to adopt a self-centered (or perhaps "us-centered") mentality which fundamentally misunderstood the meaning of their election. To be clear, this was not by any means a distinctly Jewish problem, but simply a human one. We have already addressed it in the previous chapter, where we observed the tendency to look at grace in a self-centered way and think that God has saved us simply so that we can sit at ease atop the pile of benefits he has bestowed on us. In fact, the greatest blessing God has given us is the honor of partnership with him in the temporal work of redemption and the eternal work of glory, and the gifts he gives us along the way are given to further this work. We are blessed to be a blessing. We see this plainly in Abraham's commission in Genesis 12:1–3. God promised to give him and his offspring great blessings, and also to bless all nations through them. At some points throughout their history, it seemed as though Israel rejoiced in the first part of that promise but neglected the second part. They expected protection and prosperity from God, but overlooked their mission to be a light of God's righteousness, justice, and mercy for the gentiles. They didn't always remember that their election by God called them into God's mission for the world. This is, after all, what election has always been about. Israel was always meant to be a wall, yes, but a wall built to hold a door for others into God's presence.

Seen in this context, the creation of the Jew-gentile church through the Messiah Jesus was not the denial of Israel, but the fulfillment of Israel's mission. Christianity was never meant to be a "new religion" founded by Jesus Christ to supersede Judaism. Christianity is simply fulfilled Judaism—God's covenant now open for people of all nations, on the sole basis of faith in Christ. God's people Israel and God's people the church are simply the same people inhabiting the same story, oriented around the single promise-covenant of God which is realized in Jesus Christ, for the sake of the world.[2]

This was a truth over which many stumbled in Paul's time, and many still stumble today. It was a scandal to the ethnocentric mentality of many Jews, who did not grasp that the unique blessing God had given them was for the sake of the gentiles too. To see gentiles come into the same fold of God's holy people not through circumcision or observance of the law, but simply by faith in the Messiah Jesus, challenged their idea that "we alone are the people of God."

---

2. Or as N. T. Wright has put it, God's "single-plan-through-Israel-for-the-world." Wright, *Justification*, 106.

This also was (and still is) a scandal from the gentile side of the fence. The message proclaimed to them was that the one true creator God, who rules the whole world, was not to be identified with their various deities, but was the God worshiped by the Jews, and the only way to worship this God and be counted one of his people was to respond in faith to Jesus Christ. The Jewish Messiah was proclaimed to be the savior not only for the Jews, but for the whole world, too.

These two scandals—the scandal of gentile believers entering unity with Jewish believers by faith alone, and the scandal of the Jewish Messiah as the savior for gentiles—are really the same scandal seen from opposite sides. It is once again the scandal of particularity, in which God uses the particular and the provincial to reach out universally to all the world. This offends two basic human impulses, which we have already seen in the way that Jews and gentiles were respectively scandalized by the gospel: the impulse of ethnocentrism, and the impulse of pluralism, (which will be further described below). Put in these terms, we see more clearly how the gospel of Jesus Christ still shocks the world. It bucks against both ethnocentrism and pluralism by creating a new social identity: the universal people of God through faith in Christ alone.

Circles of Solidarity

In our study of Ephesians, we have already thought much about the basic problems of the world. We've seen that there are rebellious powers waging war against God, and that we have all been complicit with these powers. Our part in this rebellion has separated us from God, and has therefore also fractured all other relationships in which God meant for us to partake. We have seen that we are all victims of this basic problem, yet we ourselves are part of the problem. Much of this can be boiled down to one simple word: pride.

Pride can be defined many ways, but at its core, it seems to be the attitude which says, "It's all about me." We insist on being the center of our world. Pride, and sin in general, means being self-centered people in a God-centered universe. As such, it is an act of denial against reality—the reality of God and the fact of our createdness.

Perhaps this seems especially pronounced in our own modern, Western, individualistic culture, in which we tend to be preoccupied with our own personal rights, freedoms, and choices. It's the kind of culture in which Frank Sinatra could sing "I did it my way" and receive many nods of approval. In some other cultures doing things "my way" might be interpreted as a shameful failure to live in harmony with the community. But the problem of self-centeredness is not by any means confined to the Western world. It is a problem which has perhaps more often taken the collective form of an "us-centeredness." This may be an improvement in many ways over individualism, but it is ultimately just a different form of the same thing. The impulse to set "me" over against "you" is just a variation of the impulse to set "us" over against "them." Ethnocentrism is a collectivized form of egocentrism; or alternatively we could say that egocentrism is an individualized form of ethnocentrism.

One way of describing this phenomenon is through what I call "circles of solidarity." By this I simply mean any group which identifies itself as an "us" in contrast to a "them." We constantly draw circles around ourselves to designate which group we belong to. This group can be called a solidarity because it thinks of itself as a unit; a collective whole to which actions and attributes can be ascribed. Endless examples can be cited. On the small end of the spectrum, every family is a circle of solidarity. On the large end are nations and empires. By those two examples, we immediately see that these circles do not necessarily exclude each other, but that large circles can include smaller ones concentrically. Circles can also overlap. For example, a few people in a community might simultaneously belong to the country club and to the bowling league (trivial examples as these might be). But other circles by nature exclude one another. National identities largely function this way. Of course there are exceptions: people do hold dual citizenships and many have overlapping senses of national identity. But perhaps most people who say "I'm an American" mean, among other things, that they are not Australian, Brazilian, Chinese, or any other nationality. It's a claimed identity which describes what we are over against what we are not. We can see this pointedly when people say things like "We are not white, black, or Latinos, we are Americans." That's a way of saying that the American national circle of solidarity should trump all other circles of solidarity—or at least ethnic ones.

It is in this exclusive sense that we are also to understand the first-century distinction between Jews and gentiles. These labels designated two non-overlapping circles of solidarity, and physical circumcision was the boundary marker. Of course, we should note that only Jews would have described it this way. No gentile would probably have referred to himself or herself as such. "Gentile" was a word used by Jews to designate non-Jews. However, non-Jewish Greeks, Romans, Syrians, or Egyptians (for example) would have clearly understood that they were not members of that unique people called the Hebrews. In short, Jews and non-Jews both possessed mutually exclusive social identities. They belonged to separate and non-overlapping circles of solidarity.

Until, that is, they became members of the Christian community. Jesus Christ alone, claims Paul, has the power to undo that division by creating a single circle of solidarity, "thus making peace." Elsewhere, Paul shows how this new identity in Christ dissolves not only the barrier between Jews and gentiles, but all kinds of divisions: "For in Christ Jesus you are all children of God through faith. As many of you who were baptized into Christ have clothed yourselves with Christ. There is no longer Jew or Greek, there is no longer slave or free, there is no longer male and female; for all of you are one in Christ Jesus" (Gal 3:26–28). Here we begin to see how God in Christ has addressed the major human problem of pride expressed in egocentrism/ethnocentrism.

We live in a world in which people and people groups seem hopelessly divided against each other. The instinct to play our "us-vs-them" games runs intractably deep. It is blatantly visible in every proud empire in world history. But the basic problem is just as present now as it ever has been, even in our age of unprecedented pluralism and globalism. We continue to see very powerful and destructive kinds of circles of solidarity emphasized through racism, arrogant nationalism, and political parties which vie for the uncontested allegiance of constituents. But the problem can be much more subtle than this, too. Against racism and nationalism, there is a strong push for a relativistic pluralism. This may seem like a fitting antidote to the problem, but in many cases, it is simply a different form of the same thing.

We can look at it this way. Ethnocentrism involves the drawing of circles which assert their superiority, dominance, and normativity over other circles. Pluralism involves the drawing of circles which keep a wide margin of distance between themselves and other circles, creating ideological buffer-zones between people groups so as to prevent one group from rudely imposing itself on another. As different as these approaches may be, they are frequently simply alternative strategies for the achievement of the same self-centered goal: to assert our own group's claim on reality and protect it from the challenges of others. Ethnocentrism does this directly, and often with hostility. But pluralism, in many cases, is simply a more polite form of ethnocentrism. When we make the claim that every group is right (a claim which in many cases is not rationally coherent), what we often really mean is, "I don't care what you think. Just leave me alone and let me think however I want." That, at its core, is a fundamentally self-centered mentality. The ethno-relativist says many polite things about the equality of all cultures and people groups, but may nonetheless privately gloat over his own enlightened vantage point. He still believes that he and his clan are superior. He's merely asserting that superiority through membership in a circle which is defined according to a modernist liberal ideology rather than an ethnic or national identity. We simply cannot get away from our destructive and dehumanizing "us-vs-them" mentalities—at least not apart from the gospel of Jesus Christ.

At this point, we need to make a clarification. Circles of solidarity are not bad in themselves. This characteristic of humanity whereby we form groups and collectivities is a feature of creation, not of the fall. There is nothing inherently wrong with tribes, nations, or other human social collectivities. As such, there is nothing wrong with the words "us" or "them." They are necessary to the nature of our existence as creatures who are both social (partaking in relational networks) and finite (we cannot be, nor should we be, equally related to all people). As we have already observed, God created us to be social creatures, living in communities which can say "we" and which can therefore refer to other communities as "them." Exclusive relationships are part of God's design, and we need to look no further than marriage to see this.

However, the mentalities of "us" and "them," necessary and innocent as they are, inevitably take on many destructive forms under the condition of human pride. They become the arena in which the powers of evil work; the polarity from which all proud and wicked empires gain their strength. We see this clearly in the biblical story of Babel, where people gathered together under a demonically powerful "we" who aspired to rise to the heavens and become as God. It occurred in the powerful mythos of *Pax Romana*, wherein constituents of the empire saw themselves as rightful members of a reigning world order. We see it in the first-century Jewish claim that "we are the circumcision," here taking a God-given membership in a circle meant to embody humble servitude with open arms to the world, and turning it into something proud and exclusive. We see it in a grotesque extreme in Hitler's Third Reich, which set up the Germanic people as the great "we" claiming superiority over "them," especially certain dehumanized others, like the Jews. We even see the same basic mentality in the mythos of American exceptionalism, in which the United States is believed to occupy a unique providential position as a city on a hill; a people uniquely endowed by God to establish new political norms of democracy around the world. This is a "we" which enjoys a boast of superiority over against the rest of the world, even if it does so in what it supposes to be a benevolent manner.[3] In all these ways and so many more, human beings have forged for themselves groups or collectivities through which they understand and assert their own unique identities.

As we have said, one apparent alternative to this is pluralism, which in its essence says to each circle, "Who are you to make yourself the center of the world?" But in saying this, pluralism simply wants to set up its own center in the world, free from the interference of others who challenge our self-centered beliefs. Pluralism is the attractive but fundamentally selfish belief that every community has the right to set itself up quietly as the center of its own universe. We see this in the gentile sense of scandal at the idea that their savior should come from Israel and not their local temple.

In the midst of this situation of clashing powers and human pride, God introduces his solution: a new circle of solidarity, founded not upon allegiance to Caesar or pagan piety, but the lordship of Jesus Christ; not upon righteous law-observance or Abrahamic descent, but the unmerited grace of God. This new circle of solidarity, the people of God in Christ, pulls together people who were previously alienated by their power-struggles and prideful group identities. As we saw, in Christ "there is neither Jew nor Gentile, slave nor free, male and female." Here being a Jew or a gentile, male or female, rich or poor, black or white, American, Chinese, or Syrian, no longer constitutes our essential identity which sets us apart from one another. All these identities, these circles of solidarity, are relativized for those who are "in Christ." Of course, they are not altogether canceled. All those identities remain significant in their own way. But in Christ, they lose their status as claims of power and superiority. They lose their power to separate us from one another and from God.

The claim of Ephesians 2 is that out of these disparate peoples who were formerly alienated from each other through their mutually exclusive allegiances, God has crafted a single people who now point uniquely to himself. This is why Paul compares the people of God in Christ to the

---

3. For a good introduction to the idea of American exceptionalism from a Christian point of view, see Wilsey, *American Exceptionalism and Civil Religion*.

temple. God's people are a temple of which Christ himself is the cornerstone. We remember that Israel's temple was always meant to signify God's dwelling place on earth; the place where God's presence and power in the world were made manifestly visible. The temple in Jerusalem was a message written to all the world, in the language of brick and mortar, that the God of Israel was Lord of all.[4] It stood as an invitation to come and worship the one true creator God. But this invitation was not without barriers. Only priests could enter the sanctuary, and only male Jews of good standing (cleanliness, in Levitical language) could enter the inner court. Women and God-fearing gentiles were excluded to the outer regions of the temple complex.

The gentiles had temples of their own, of course. Ephesus was home to the temple of the goddess Artemis. Indeed, many major cities in the Greco-Roman world boasted a temple or shrine of some sort to a patron deity. Besides their obvious function as houses of idolatrous worship, such temples were objects of local pride. They formed centers of local circles of solidarity; focal points for a local group's sense of shared identity. There is in fact a deep connection between human circles of solidarity and idolatry. Many of our circles, in the context of human pride, are treated as though they were ultimate reality. When our fundamental and final sense of identity is rooted in our nationality, for example, we are raising something that is valid but ultimately a human construct to the level of ultimate reality. Perhaps many of our human communities are centered around idolatrous temples in this sense, whether or not a physical shrine is present. We all gravitate toward the tendency to center our lives and our identities around something that is not, in fact, the center; something which we have set up and in which we can take pride; something in whose name we can exclude or dominate other groups.

But God has built a new and final temple: Jesus Christ together with those who are in union with him through faith. It is through this Christ, and through this people, that God has fully asserted his redemptive rule over all things. Here in Christ, all people are able to enter the presence of God to worship, and this constitutes the true ground of human fellowship. Worship—the enjoyment of God's love and the expression of our love in return—is our fundamental human vocation, and through this alone

---

4. This message would be just another proud claim of dominance apart from the conviction that the God who revealed himself to Israel and was incarnate in Jesus Christ truly exists as the creator of all, and therefore alone claims rightful lordship over all things. That is a presupposition apart from which nothing I have written—or indeed, Paul has written—can stand.

can we fully enjoy human fellowship together. Here alone can we return to the circle in which we were created, which is defined by God's love for all people; a love which conditions all our social and vocational relations. Indeed, this new temple is also the original and only valid one, for it alone is grounded on the reality of God and his creational purposes for us.

The Scandal of Unity

Now we can finally get around to addressing the scandal of all this. The phrase "scandal of unity" may be an odd one, because at first glance, nothing seems less scandalous than unity. Everybody likes unity. Who doesn't desire world peace? Even those who cynically mock the desire for peace and unity will not be shocked by it, but treat it is as something silly and naïve, perhaps with a sarcastic comment about singing "Kumbaya" around a campfire. Unity might be regarded as unrealistic, but "scandalous" hardly seems the word.

Until, that is, we consider what it really involves. Paul's claim in Ephesians is that the whole world is fractured through the condition of rebellion against God along with powers and principalities which are hostile to him. But God is actively involved in putting this fragmented creation back together, and the mending of human divisions is a crucial part of this large-scale saving work. The only way any of this is accomplished is through Jesus Christ, the one in whom all things have ultimate unity. The only place where we can find true unity and peace is in a common solidarity with Jesus Christ.

Consider what this means: if Jesus is the center, nothing else is. Unity is accomplished by entering a new circle of solidarity in Christ, in which allegiance to him supersedes all the allegiances of our old circles. For the powers-that-be, this is a scandal of the highest order. It meant, for ancient inhabitants of Roman Empire like the Ephesians, that Caesar was not be called "lord." It also meant the end of their worship of locally venerated deities. It meant, for first-century Jews, that circumcision and the law of Moses, their ultimate rule of life, had reached its fulfillment in the person of Jesus Christ and therefore must give way to faith in him as their basis for understanding their covenantal relationship with God.

It means many similar things for us now, too. Our unity in the circle defined by Jesus Christ means that our ultimate allegiance does not belong to the claims of blood, soil, and nation, those affections which pull so strongly on our hearts. Our membership in the circle of Jesus Christ supersedes our membership in the circles of our political interest groups. For Christians in my country, it supersedes our membership in that powerful circle we call America. Our ultimate identity and loyalty do not belong to kin, king, or country, but Christ alone. That is the scandal.

There is an important clarification on this point, however. All of us, as Ephesians 2 makes clear, have been rebels against God, and part of the rebellion involves our loyalties to powers other than God. But in the reversal of this situation, where we become members of God's household, we do not therefore become rebels against the state. That is how the game is played in the world: if you are mine, you will fight against my enemies. But that is not how God's kingdom works. If we belong to the Lord, we will learn to love our enemies, because it is only according to this love that we ourselves have been redeemed. That is why elsewhere (Romans 13, for example) Paul commands his audience to live in humble submission to the reigning worldly powers. This is not an endorsement of those powers. It is not a return to the veneration of Caesar. It is imitation of the servant, who brought redemption by dying for his persecutors; who used some of his final breaths to say "Forgive them, Father, for they know not what they do." Perhaps that is a kind of rebellion after all. It is the revolt of love against the powers of hate. We make the loudest protest against those who persecute us when we say "I love you anyway."

There's another point to be made here as well. Membership in the circle of solidarity created by God in Christ does not mean the abolishment of our membership in all other circles. The Ephesians who believed did not cease to be Ephesians. The Jews who believed did not cease to be Jews. Although Paul boldly says in Galatians that in Christ there is no Jew or gentile, slave or free, male and female, of course those facts about members of his audience did not simply disappear. He meant that those identity markers were no longer definitive for their relation to God or one another. They no longer had the power to separate and divide. In the same way, Americans (for example) who are Christians do not by any means cease to be Americans. But their membership in the kingdom of God is what ultimately defines their identity, allegiance, values, and behavior, not their American citizenship.

This does not mean that any Christian should cease to love his or her country. It is actually quite the opposite. Christians ought to be the best citizens, but on an entirely different basis than those whose loyalty ultimately belongs to the kingdoms of this world. We do not cease to participate in our old circles, but, according to our ultimate allegiance to Jesus Christ, we participate in them in an entirely new way. First-century Jews who became followers of Jesus did not reject their Jewish identity, but realized that this identity as God's child had been fully actualized in Christ. Ephesians did not reject their status as Ephesians, but inhabited that identity in a radically new way.

So too for Christians now in twenty-first-century America. We are to love our country not because we believe that she is the best country in the world, but because she is—just like the rest of the world—a collectivity of sinful people who are deeply loved by God; people whom Christ died to save. Our country, and indeed our entire world, is one great neighborhood inhabited by people who are, for us, the object of the second-greatest commandment: to love our neighbors as ourselves. In this sense, we can truly say that God loves America more than we do; far more than the most ardent patriot. But he does not love her because she is America. He loves her in precisely the same way as he loves the whole world: as a race of lost but deeply beloved sinners; image-bearers of God who have rebelled against him, but whom he desires to redeem.

Christians are therefore called to be good citizens of our countries, as well as faithful members of our families and communities, but in a unique way which the world finds scandalous: on the basis of an undivided loyalty to Jesus Christ.[5] The powers of our world clamor for our allegiance. They

---

5. Soren Kierkegaard wrote a book with the intriguing title *Purity of Heart Is To Will One Thing*. Here is a helpful way of thinking about the singularity of our loyalty to Jesus Christ. Purity of heart is indeed to will one thing, but by willing the one right thing, we will thereby also will all good things. To will the one right thing is not to reject the world, but to affirm all that is good in it. If we will what God wills and love what he loves, then our willing one thing will not exclude our love for one another, or for our families, for good earthy pleasures, or for our human communities, but will include them together in a new way, completely oriented around the purposes of God. This is part of our Christian answer to the question of the one and the many, which we looked at in chapter 1. Even as unity and plurality coexist in the Trinity, so all reality is a dance of union and difference, in which the one contains the many without denying or destroying or dissolving them into its unity. In the same way, orienting ourselves toward a singular love and loyalty to God will not mean a denial of all people, places, or things, but rather an affirmation of them by seeing them in light of our relationship with God. Yet that relationship with God is exclusive in the sense that it alone establishes the context and agenda for all other relationships and identities. Martin Buber makes much the same point when he says that the authentic, I-Thou relation to God "fills the firmament—not as though there were nothing else, but everything else lives in its light" (Buber, *I and Thou*, 126).

demand that we see the world as from the center of their circles, and orient our lives around their agendas. But we deny the ultimacy of those things the world calls ultimate. We see all our relationships and memberships in the world singularly through the light of the gospel of Jesus Christ. We love our nation more than any nationalist and the world more than any humanitarian, not on account of their deservingness nor any greatness in ourselves, but simply because we love the world on God's terms rather than its own. Insofar as we do this, we are a scandalous people.

Conclusion

It is popular (perhaps even cliché) to say that all humans are ultimately brothers and sisters, a single family and race. It's a claim that is made by many who long for peace and unity in the world. But only in the scriptural story of creation is there a foundation for such a claim, and only in the redemption brought about by Christ is there hope for its actualization.

Against this, there are many competing strategies for how to achieve such unity. One is unity through conformity to the powerful and arrogant. This is the way of ethnocentrism: "Be united by becoming like us." It is the solution posed by every proud empire. It is unity at the expense of love and respect—indeed, at the expense of humanity.

Another strategy is unity through pluralism, where we say, "Be united by being true to yourself and giving everyone else space to do the same." This may be less overtly destructive than the previous option, but it really is just as self-centered. It is unity at the expense of integrity and commitment to the truth, and there is no ground for authentic unity outside of the truth.

But God's strategy is: "Be united by being joined to Jesus Christ." This is not unity on the basis of human pride or self-determination, but unity grounded in the great truths of creation and redemption. Only in God, the source and goal of all things, is there real unity and peace. Only in Christ, who is our mediator and savior, can the walls set up by rebellious allegiances and prideful wills be torn down. Only here, through the cross, can God's temple rise; the temple which is the declaration (in and through redeemed sinners) of God's redeeming presence in the world.

Heavenly Father, we praise you for making us your children, and that by bringing us into your family, you have created peace. Thank you for being the wise creator and loving redeemer, for we know that here alone is hope for

The Scandal of Unity

our world. And what great hope we have! It is not a hope hanging uncertainly before us, but one already created in your son, Jesus Christ. We know that even as he has certainly died and been raised, that we are your people and that you are our God.

Father, may we therefore love one another and seek the peace of our broken world. As Christ is our peace, may we, living in him, be the peace of the world. But give us, O Lord, the courage to confront the divisions and lies of the world with the sharp-edged truth of the gospel. Deliver us from false contentment with powers that are not your power and love that is not your love. May you, by the power of your love, tear down those divisions among us—divisions of race and blood and soil—and dissolve the unions among us which are founded on anything besides the cross of your Christ. Lead us away from these idolatries of the world, and make us a temple where your name alone is proclaimed. In the power of the Spirit and the name of the Son do we pray this, Father. Amen.

5

The Scandal of God's Human Project

Paraphrase: Ephesians 3:1–13

THIS IS THE REASON *that I, Paul, am a prisoner for Christ Jesus. It is for your sake, Gentiles. For you must already know that I have been commissioned by God's grace on your behalf. Therefore, you also know how the mystery was revealed to me, as I have already written. In reading this, you will be able to understand my insight into the mystery of Christ. This mystery was not revealed to humankind in previous generations, but it has now been revealed by the Spirit to God's holy apostles and prophets. The mystery, now revealed, is that the Gentiles have become fellow heirs with Israel, members of the same body, and participants together in the promise, which is yours in Jesus Christ through the gospel.*

I have become a servant of this gospel, by the gift of God's grace, which was given to me by the working of his power. Although I am the very least among all God's holy people, this is his grace to me: that I would bring the revelation of the boundless riches of Christ to the Gentiles; to uncover before all eyes the mystery which for ages had been known only to the creator of all. In this way, God has demonstrated his multi-faceted wisdom, through his church, before the rulers and authorities in the heavenly realms. This is his eternal purpose, which was accomplished in Christ Jesus our Lord. Through faith in him, we can approach God with boldness and confidence. Therefore, this is my prayer: that you may not lose heart because of my sufferings for you, because my ministry to you, even in suffering, is the glory of God made available to you.

The Scandal of God's Human Project

In the last two chapters of Ephesians, Paul has talked a lot of theology. He has explained much about God's eternal purposes, established in creation and fulfilled in the redemption worked by Jesus Christ. He has reminded his audience of their own relationship to these great truths: that we are all by our own nature related negatively to the work of God because of our sin and rebellion against him, but that we come back into the fold of God's glorious purposes by entering union with Jesus Christ through faith. This message is not without scandal in the present world, in which we are surrounded by the devices of selfish pride and idolatrous allegiances to the powers which remain in rebellion against God and which divide us from one another.

Here in chapter 3, Paul's message takes a profoundly personal turn. For Paul, these great theological truths are not merely matters of his teaching curriculum. They are the bedrock of his own personal sense of identity and mission as an apostle, and they frame all his relationships. Paul's self-understanding, rooted as it is not in himself but in his savior, here seeks to spill over into the lives of his readers so that they too understand their role in God's great drama.

But for all the personal and relational concern at work in this passage, it is not for a moment less theologically profound. On the contrary, it is here in this passage that Paul perhaps most clearly gets to the heart of the great questions: the questions of divine purpose and human existence, and how they intersect in the life of God's people through Jesus Christ. Indeed, we have now come to the crux of the matter: God's purpose in the created universe involves—scandalously—manifesting his eternal wisdom through finite and fallen human beings. This is the profound idea we are invited to explore.

The Wisdom of God

Let's begin with a question: was God wise in creating this world?

First, there was nothing but God. Father, Son, and Holy Spirit. Three persons, one being, in perfect joy and satisfaction within the trinitarian communion. This was all that there was—and all was perfect. And yet, God decided to make something which was not himself; something else that would have being, but which would be distinct from him. Not only this: he decided that in his created universe there would be persons other than himself. They would have wills which were not identical with his own.

Their actions would not be God's actions by instrumental extension, as my brain acts through my hand, but causally and morally attributable to them. They would be capable of agreeing with God. But they would therefore also be capable of disagreeing with him, even rebelling against him. God made a creature which could love and obey and believe him—and therefore one which could also, if it so chose, spit in his face. He created a creature capable of displaying the divine image: the manifestation, in some small measure, of his goodness, intelligence, and love. But by this he risked the misuse of this capacity, which would fill the world with evil and hatred. Was it worth it for God to delegate his power for the sake of love? Was God wise in creating this world?

We see how the story unfolds. God creates children made in his image; the children revolt and become his enemies. This, of course, was part of the risk. Evil begets evil, and soon God himself says that he regrets creating the world and that it must be almost destroyed through a catastrophic flood. If that is how bad things turned out, was God wise in creating this world?

But although God almost destroyed the world, he did not give up on it. He persisted in seeking redemption, and he did this through a people: the children of Israel. He called these people his very own, and brought them out of slavery in Egypt with a mighty hand and outstretched arm. He led them to his holy mountain in the wilderness where they beheld his glory. But there they rebelled and worshiped a golden calf. God said he would destroy this people, and relented only at the intercession of his servant Moses. Was God wise in creating this people?

God, in astonishing mercy, worked with his sinful people and brought them into the promised land. There he established them and made them prosper. But they turned aside from the worship of their creator to worship created things: fallen heavenly beings, earthly empires, even the work of their own hands. In anger and sorrow God banished his people to exile. The people through whom he purposed to bring redemption from the world's problems turned out to be part of the problem themselves. Was God wise in making humans the instruments of his redeeming work?

In spite of the failure of his people to live up to their calling, God persisted in his redemption project. He sent prophet after prophet to call the people to repentance and faith. Mostly they were ignored. Many were persecuted. Some were killed. At last, God came himself, when the Father sent the Son into the world. And the world nailed him to a cross.

The Scandal of God's Human Project

Was God wise in creating this world? What exactly is God up to in this universe? Does he know what he is doing, or is he the simply the great improvisor, making it all up as he goes along? Does he have some secret cards up his sleeve?

These are questions which haunt us. They are, to invoke Paul's term, mysterious. They comprise the mystery with which people of faith have always had to deal, as they have stumbled forward in the confidence that despite so many feelings and appearances to the contrary, God is infinitely good, loving, and wise. Lest we think that these questions are impious for us to ask, we need to be reminded that they are the very realm in which faith dwells. Yes, faith answers them in the affirmative. But this presupposes the fact that people of faith do indeed ask them.

But we aren't the only ones asking. The world at large, insofar as it believes in God at all, shakes its head at him. This is visible in the problem of evil, in which we ponder how God—if there is a God—can possibly co-exist with the all the suffering and general dysfunction we see in the world. Many think that it is preferable not to believe in God than to be confronted with the mystery of his way in the world. The mystery of the wisdom of God is pondered, then, both by people of faith and by many other people in the world.

And then, it is also pondered by—well, *others*. Throughout Ephesians, we meet a set of mysterious characters: rulers, authorities, powers, dominions, spirits of the air. Paul discusses them a bit more concretely in chapter 6, but we will deal with that later. Here we are told that God is revealing his wisdom before the "rulers and authorities in the heavenly realms." It is a cryptic comment. We are perhaps helped a little by 1 Peter 1:10–12, in which the disciple explains how believers stand at the receiving end of truths which even angels long to understand. The same idea is conveyed elegantly in Charles Wesley's great hymn, *And Can It Be that I Should Gain*:

> Tis mystery all! The Immortal dies!
> Who can explore his strange design?
> In vain the firstborn seraph tries
> To sound the depths of live divine!
> Tis mercy all! Let earth adore,
> Let angel mends inquire no more.[1]

---

1. Wesley, *And Can It Be that I Should Gain*.

We can imagine the angelic beings present at the creation of the space-time universe and observing the spectacle as if from a grandstand. Perhaps many of them scratch their heads (anthropomorphically speaking, of course), utterly puzzled by the sheer novelty of it all. Perhaps this is a far-fetched fantasy—it may very well be the case that angelic beings were created alongside the space-time universe at least partly for the purpose of carrying out some of God's purposes within it (Hebrews 1:14 might suggest this).

But in any case, we can imagine the angelic head-scratching to intensify when God creates human creatures, beings bound to him and his will only by the fragile thread of love set free. Perhaps murmurings ensued among the heavenly court as to whether God was truly wise in governing the world with so long a leash. God had created a being which was capable of rebelling against him. Why take such a risk? Why do such a foolish thing?

This may be more speculation than we are warranted to indulge in, but the book of Job seems to give us an invitation to entertain these kinds of thoughts. There we glimpse an exchange between God and Lucifer in the heavenly courtroom. Lucifer thinks that humans even at their best (the man Job being the case in point) only glorify God because he blesses them—basically, because they are paid for their worship. What is implied here is Satan's skepticism about the very nature of God's human project. God has created humans with freedom and personal self-hood. Will such beings ever worship and obey God simply for who he is, without threat, payment, or compulsion? Isn't it inevitable that such personal freedom will only result in selfishness and rebellion? The great conflagration of evil which has erupted in the world seems to suggest so. And if even an apparently righteous man like Job can be made to curse God if his blessings are taken away, doesn't this confirm all the more that God's whole idea of creating a world of freedom is a failure? The ensuing story of Job is one in which Lucifer's point of view is proved wrong. God does succeed, at the very least, in getting one good man.[2]

While we must exercise appropriate theological modesty in the face of such claims, Ephesians 3 certainly suggests that there is a dispute among heavenly powers regarding the wisdom of God and the mystery of his way in the world. This passage also tells us that God has an answer up his sleeve; a tour-de-force argument to silence his opponents. What is that answer?

---

2. I owe this perspective on Job to Fredrickson, *Creation and Creation's God*, 3–8.

The Scandal of God's Human Project

In short, the answer is *us*. The mystery of God—his plan of redemption for the world by which his wisdom as creator will be vindicated—turns out to be a people; his church. God is staking this all (as he did in the book of Job) on the frail foundation of human faith.

To do such a thing looks foolish, and it absolutely would be foolish were it not for the brilliant centerpiece of God's strategy: the person of Jesus Christ. The question is "Was God wise in creating this world?" It's a question which winds through the whole scriptural narrative, and it receives a resounding "yes" in the person of Jesus Christ, the eternal logos or wisdom of God. And the astonishing good news of the gospel is that through faith in him, God's people inhabit this glorious "yes" he has spoken in Jesus Christ. In solidarity with him, we as God's people are the vindication of his wisdom.

Once again, we think about the angelic grandstand, in which countless celestial beings (some on God's side, others not) look into the arena in which God's drama plays out. Will this whole project of creating a world populated with people capable of faith, hope, and love pan out? Or will it only yield unbelief, despair, and hatred? For millennia, it all looked like a fool's errand, save for a few unusual characters here and there (the sort which are listed in Hebrews 11). But at a moment in history which could not have been predicted from anyone living within it, God's plan—the mystery—is revealed. The card comes out of his sleeve. The chess piece makes the crushing move upon which the entire game had been secretly staked. Victory is declared after a long string of defeats which turn out, in retrospect, to have been a great series of strategic movements.

It is a victory won by God in Christ, and an achievement for which we cannot claim the slightest credit. And yet, by grace through faith, we are participants in it, and not even in a marginal, along-for-the-ride kind of sense. Human beings are at the center of God's eternal plan for the universe.[3] We have all strayed far from the center through our own rebellion.

---

3. We should note how this way of framing things gets around the false dichotomies which are sometimes placed between human-centeredness versus God-centeredness. In fact there is, unfortunately, a great deal of human-centered theology at large in which God is thought to exist largely to make us comfortable. But Scripture's presentation of the situation is human-centered and majestically God-centered at the same time, for the reason that God in his grace has chosen to create the universe in such a way that human creatures are important to his plan. God alone is inherently great and glorious; apart from him we are absolutely nothing. But he has decided, by his grace alone, that we should not be apart from him, but rather drawn into his glory.

But the center has been reclaimed by Jesus Christ, and insofar as we are drawn into union with him, we stand there once again.

Perhaps we can say this more plainly. What God has always wanted to create is a people who would be holy and blameless before him (Eph 1:4): a people of faith, hope, and love. But these are things which not even omnipotence can create by force. They can only be a free response to loving initiative. This is inherently risky, but a world without this risk would be a world, by necessity, without faith, hope, and love; a world without real persons. God, like the craftsman from the *Pinocchio* story, can make himself puppets aplenty, but what he wants is a real boy, capable of real love—and therefore also real mischief. Of these possibilities, the human race has collectively embraced the latter. But real God-glorifying humanity is something that God has now created by becoming human himself in Jesus Christ, and he invites us to partake in it by faith. In and through Christ, we (God's church) are the realization of God's purposes in creation. This is a truth at once staggeringly glorious and completely humbling: glorious because we are now, in Christ, the shining centerpiece of God's creation project by which his wisdom is put on display before the hosts of heaven; humbling because we are only in this spotlight of grace and glory because Christ has pulled us onto the stage to share it with him, through his self-sacrificial mercy alone and not through an ounce of our own merit.

A Christ-Centered Humanism

God's purpose in creation (to showcases his goodness, wisdom, and love) has always involved a plan to create a people; to assemble a society of human image-bearers. This project is realized in the supreme divine-human image-bearer Jesus Christ and those who are in union with him through faith: the church. In short, God has chosen to manifest his wisdom through created, finite, human beings. This is really quite shocking, and no less so for the reason that God has made it possible by stepping in to succeed where we failed by becoming human himself. This is very surprising from any number of vantage points. How could—and why would—God become human? And, to our present point, why would he seek to accomplish his goals in the first place through puny, fallible human beings?

"Being human" has, at least in certain quarters, a decidedly negative connotation. In many religious and philosophical traditions, being human is almost like an illness; a condition which must somehow be cured or

The Scandal of God's Human Project

overcome. In many Eastern religions and philosophies, those things which we chiefly associate with our humanity, such as a bodily, personal, individual existence in which we desire certain things, is a great illusion which must be dispelled by realizing the truth that all is one. Much of the Greek philosophical tradition which has so strongly influenced the Western world is actually in agreement with this point. In particular, the tradition of Neoplatonism is decidedly biased against all things physical and bodily. Here one of the chief goals of human existence is to escape the body with all its crude needs and desires, to learn to look beyond the physical world of time and change (regarded as illusory or less than fully real), and to enjoy an eternal contemplation of the rational world of pure, unchanging ideas. Here every part of the human person but his or her rationality must go. Our humanity—such as it involves bodily activities and emotional longings—are mere shadows cast against the wall of Plato's cave.[4] We must leave them behind and enter the great daylight of pure thought.

This philosophical perspective has been very influential on Christianity throughout its history. In Augustine, for example, we find a strong influence from Platonism: we need to leave behind the desires and pleasures of bodily existence, and pursue the eternal contemplation of the supreme spiritual good, which is God. Augustine was suspicious of all bodily enjoyments (food, music, sex, etc.) as troublesome distractions at best and idolatrous lusts at worst. This way of looking at things has trickled down through many Christian traditions. Our humanity is something which is often regarded as something either to be overcome by moralistic, ascetic effort, or covered over by grace (or some combination of both). We see the first route in many monastic traditions, where holy men and women leave the world in pursuit of a purely spiritual life.[5] We also see it in the form of various legalistic habits of mind which crop up from time to time, in which

---

4. Plato created a memorable analogy by comparing human existence to the plight of persons trapped inside a deep cave, in which they face a wall which is lit by a fire and features the shadows cast by statues. The cave-dwellers mistake this show of light-and-shadows for reality, when what they need is to escape the cave and enter the world of daylight. This process of leaving the cave may be compared to enlightenment in Eastern thought, or to conversion in Western religion (Plato, *Republic*, 240–48). We can see a vivid contemporary retelling of this story in the movie *The Matrix*, in which people think that they are leading ordinary lives when they are really inside a giant computer program, and must choose to take a pill to allow them to awake from their virtual dreams.

5. This is not meant to discredit all monasticism or spiritual, ascetic practices. For those who are called to such vocations, they are a great good, insofar as they are understood as a way of being human before God rather than as an escape from our humanity.

the main point of being a Christian seems to be abstaining from a list of certain worldly activities. We see the second route (our humanity covered over by grace) undertaken in systems of sacramental theology, in which grace is sometimes viewed as a spiritual substance which is communicated to us through various church practices, or else in non-sacramental understandings of grace, in which it is viewed as a God-ordained excuse for our sorry condition of being merely human. In all these understandings, the final destiny of redeemed humanity is envisioned as entrance into a spirit world, where we leave time, space, and bodily existence completely behind.

This is all very different from what we find in Scripture. It begins with a creation account in which God delights in making a physical world and reaches its climax in the making of bodily creatures capable of knowing and loving God and each other. Here God rejoices in what he has made and says that it is "very good." The scriptural canon concludes not with an immaterial spirit world, but a bodily resurrection into the new heavens and the new earth. God's revelation to us—and the whole Hebrew worldview which was shaped according to God's covenant relationship with the children of Abraham—is not interested in separating the human person into the components of body and spirit, and certainly not celebrating the latter at the expense of the former. Many people, such as Augustine, have done so, presumably with pious and honorable intentions. But we pay God no complements by disparaging his handiwork. It turns out that the rejection of the bodily aspects of human life is often built on a false dichotomy between the glorification of God and involvement in earthly activities. But God's design for human existence is that we will glorify him precisely in and through our embodied tasks and relationships. His purpose for us is not that we will escape our physical humanity, but rather for us to be human according to his creational intentions for us. God actually wants us to enjoy food, drink, music, work, art, sex, family life, and the society of our fellow humans (although of course each of them according to their God-given function and degree; as future chapters of Ephesians will show, Christianity means liberty but not libertinism).

This is the fact which Ephesians 3:10 affirms and celebrates: that God's wisdom is vindicated in and through a society of human persons, remade after the pattern of the God-man Jesus Christ. Therefore, we might well say that Christianity is in fact a Christ-centered humanism. It is the means by which we once again become fully human according to God's creation purposes, through the paradigm of humanity which has been established on our behalf in Jesus Christ.

It is not without some danger, however, that we invoke the word *humanism*, a term which has a life and history all its own, at once rich, grand, and devious. Humanism is that great project of modernity which has profoundly shaped life and thought in the Western world for the past five hundred years. It is a philosophy which was summed up eloquently a few thousand years earlier by Pythagoras in his famous statement that "Man is the measure of all things." It is a worldview which blossomed into the enlightenment project by which humanity has sought to shake off the religious authorities which governed us in the past and take charge of our own destiny through autonomous reason, emancipated societies and individuals, and world-shaping technology.

Although enlightenment humanism shapes countless aspects of life in the modern world, these three (knowledge, society/morality, and technology) are particularly significant. First, humanism shapes us epistemologically with regard to our search for truth. Here we seek to understand ourselves and our universe not through revelation or authority, but rather autonomous human reason. This approach to knowledge seems to result in two kinds of postures, each of which conflicts with the other. On the one hand, it elevates science, the study of material things, to the status of supreme arbiter of truth. Science is usually seen to be a collective social endeavor; a solidified body of knowledge which we are enjoined to unquestioningly believe. On the other hand, the ideal of autonomous reason assumes that every individual ought to have their own opinion on everything, without being told what to believe by anyone. But in either case, we as humans are responsible for what we know. Truth is not found by receiving something from God, but is won by our own initiative.

Secondly, humanism also shapes us socially and morally. One of the great myths of the enlightenment is that the human species as a whole is growing through stages of life analogous to an individual person. We had our infancy as prehistoric cave-dwellers, a time which is now to us only a dream beyond our dimmest memory. In ancient and medieval times, we were like children, clinging to nursery rhymes about gods and spirits. Finally came the renaissance and enlightenment, our adolescence and coming-of-age in which we finally grew up, learned to think for ourselves, and above all, to live on our own apart from restrictive parental rules (by this account, we have now left Plato's cave to stand in the great daylight of human reason). Now we have emancipated societies, set free to live in an equality according to "the consent of the governed." To be clear, enlightenment humanism is very far from being immoral. It is in fact the establishment of a social moral order, intended to maintain a peaceful way of life together.[6] But it is a very different kind of moral order than the sort in which (for example) medieval people lived, in which right and wrong were written into the very framework of ultimate reality. With humanism, we certainly have rules. We want them to be good rules and for everybody to follow them. But we want them to be rules which, are, fundamentally, created by our own consent.

Thirdly, humanism is technological. To the degree that they have used tools, all human societies in history have been technological. But modernity has amplified this practice into a way of looking at the world which partly defines the modern worldview. Whereas people in many times and places have sought to live in harmony with the world by adjusting and cooperating with it, the modern, Western world has taken it upon itself to reshape the world to fit our own needs, by means of our technological prowess.

In summary: through knowledge, social morality, and technology, modern humanity has (so it seems) thrown off its old restraints and ascended to its place on the throne. We have cast down the gods and risen to take their place. The humanism which typically defines our outlook on the world may not always so obviously carry this attitude of brazen hubris. But at least the seed of it is deeply ingrained in the modern, Western worldview. It is also true that we owe modernist humanism much gratitude, as it has helped create the free and equal societies in which we enjoy living, has yielded fantastic scientific discoveries, and has generally made life much safer and more comfortable. But it has all come at a great cost; a cost the value of which has become obscure to us: the knowledge that God, not humanity, is the center of the universe.

This is why we have good reason to be suspicious about the word *humanism*. We have seen how it is, from the Christian point of view, nothing else but the human revolt against God; the creature shaking its fist against its creator, insisting that now the universe must revolve around us. But if Christianity is true—if there is indeed a wise creator God and we are his creatures—then any such humanism is, in fact, radically destructive to our own humanity. If there is a creator, then it is he, not us, who knows best what kind of a creature we are and how we will best flourish. We can only

---

6. So argues Charles Tayler in *A Secular Age*.

rightly understand ourselves and the world we live in if we trustingly receive what God has chosen to reveal through his own covenantal actions in human history. We only rightly understand right and wrong in the context of his creational purposes for us. A common relation to God is, in the long run, the only possible ground for harmonious relations with each other (as Ephesians 2:11–22 shows). And we can only live in harmony with the natural world by respecting the kind of thing God has created it to be in relation to what he has created us to be.

In short, if Christianity is true, it satisfies all the demands of humanism better than humanism itself can. Paradoxically, we do not attain happiness and fulfillment and flourishing by putting ourselves at the center of all things, but by living out our humanity in light of the truth that God alone occupies that center. This is what the Old Testament writers meant when they said that "The fear of the Lord is the beginning of wisdom."

Conclusion

Unfortunately, the human condition is such that we instinctively place ourselves at the center. This is, after all, no mere invention of modernity. It is simply one more appearance of the old lie whispered in the garden: "You shall be like God!" In believing this lie, we have not only forgotten who God is. We have thereby also forgotten what it means to be truly human. There is only one way in which we can return from our exile in which we are estranged from both God and from our own humanity: through the person of Jesus Christ, who is himself both perfect divinity and unspoiled humanity. Here alone is God's purpose for us realized: in the God-centered humanism which has been embodied by Jesus Christ and in which we may participate through faith in him.

This is the supreme vindication of God's wisdom in creating the world and populating it with such odd creatures as ourselves. Here we find a surprising way of framing the identity and mission of the church: we are the community of the truly-human through Christ. It is a great mystery, but one which we are privileged to know from the inside, and from this standpoint to put it on display as we preach and embody the gospel of Jesus Christ in the world.

Heavenly Father, we give you thanks for making us human. Thank you that you have made us a little lower than the angels, rulers over the creatures of the earth. Thank you for making us powerful in our own measure: responsible before you, yet finite; working meaningfully on this earth, but without its weight upon our shoulders. Make us content with our humanity, O Lord, rejoicing in what you have made us to be, and so much more than that, in what you are.

Lord, we are thankful that we are not at the center of all things, but that you are. We are astonished by the grace in which you have made us, feeble creatures of clay, a part of your plan and showpieces of your wisdom. We know that we do not for a moment live up this calling. We praise you for living up to it for us in Jesus Christ, and we thank you that through him, we can once again become truly human before you. By the power of the Holy Spirit, may your wisdom shine in us as you work in and through us in this world.

Most of all, Lord, we praise you for your own infinite wisdom and glory, in comparison with which all things are dim, yet which by your love illuminate them all. How great are the depths of your wisdom and knowledge, O God! How unsearchable are your judgements, and your plans beyond all tracing out. Who has known your mind, O Lord? Who has given you counsel? Who has ever given to you, that you should repay them? For from you, and through you, and to you are all things. To you be the glory forever! Amen.

6

The Scandal of Love

Paraphrase: Ephesians 3:14–21

FOR THIS REASON, *I bow in prayer before the Father, from whom fatherhood itself is derived. I pray that out of his glorious riches he will strengthen you in your inner being through the power of the Holy Spirit. I pray that Christ will dwell within you through faith as you continue to be rooted and grounded in his love. I pray that you, along with all God's holy people, may have the power to grasp the immeasurably great dimensions of Christ's love, in all its width, length, height, and depth—that is, that you will be enabled to know that which surpasses knowledge. Then you will be filled with the very fullness of God. Now to him whose power is at work within us, and who by that power is able to accomplish things extravagantly beyond our greatest desires and imaginings—to him be glory forever and ever, through his holy people in Christ Jesus for all generations. Amen.*

The previous passage (Eph 3:1–13) is a great declaration of divine purpose: God's purpose of demonstrating his wisdom through creation and redemption, how God's people in Christ are inhabitants and enactors of this purpose, and how the apostle Paul understands his own life, ministry, and relationships in accordance with this purpose. Here, as in chapter 1, cosmic purpose explodes into personal prayer. Ephesians 3:14–21 is one of the most glorious prayers in all Scripture. Paul prays that his audience, having grasped the mystery of God's salvation which now defines their identity, will be able fully grasp the monumental import of this reality.

The specific content of Paul's prayer is that the Ephesians will have the power to grasp the fulness of Christ's love. Paul prays that the power of God, which is already at work on their behalf, will be at work within them to help them understand the depth of the reality in which they already live as God's adopted children. The idea that it takes supernatural power just to grasp the size of God's love is a surprising one. One of the first songs we learn as children is "Jesus loves me, this I know, for the Bible tells me so." How can that be so hard to understand?

But the love of God is not such a simple idea as we tend to suppose. It is a doctrine which at one level can be grasped by the beautiful simplicity of a little child, but on another level remains beyond the full grasp of the most learned and insightful theologian. We realize this as we attempt to understand God's love in the context of everything else God reveals about himself. All of Scripture (and Ephesians alone) tells a rich story of God's power, holiness, and glory. How does his love fit into all this? That is the challenge which stands before us. Yet Paul's prayer is that his audience—then and now—will have the power to grasp this love. Knowing that Paul did not pray in vain, that is what we will attempt to do (within our own very great limitations, of course).

Love and Power

As we have already noted, Ephesians 1:15–23 draws our attention to the relationship between God's power and his love. There we saw that his power cannot be understood apart from his love, for his power is put to work for loving purposes. God's very act of creating the universe, since it cannot be connected to any inner need within God, must be seen as an overflow of generous, agape love. Psalm 62:11 describes this connection eloquently: "One thing God has spoken, two things I have heard: power belongs with you, God, and with you, Lord, is unfailing love." The psalmist says that he knows two things for sure about God: that he is strong, and that he is loving. God's power is "power-for." It is strength in the service of love. But there is also another side to this. God's love is not merely an affectionate disposition which he feels toward other beings. It is a commitment to the absolute good, backed up by almighty power. Yes, God is benevolent, but his is a strong and fierce benevolence. God's love is a sword—but a sword on which he himself has fallen.

The Scandal of Love

What Christ did for us upon the cross shows us, as nothing else can, what love is. And it also shows us that God's love and his power are not related just as corollaries. It turns out that in some sense, God's love is his power, and his power is his love. The fact that human sexual love is procreative is a dim parable of this reality. The power by which God created the heavens and the earth is the power of love. It is the power by which an infinite being decides not to be all that there is. Surely the act of creation was, and remains, an astounding feat of divine omnipotence. But it is an omnipotence acting for purposes which are all about self-sacrificial generosity. In this respect, the creation itself anticipates the cross. God did not reinvent himself at Calvary. It was there that he put on display for all to see that which he has always been: self-emptying love. This means that while God's power certainly includes his omnipotence, it is also more than that. It is a power which is not limited to force and fiat. The power of love can create realities of which the mightiest tyrant knows nothing. As we saw in the previous chapter, creating such realities has always been God's goal. In Christ, he has created a flesh-and-blood people who know him and walk with him by faith and obedience. That is not something which can be had by omnipotence alone. It can only be won through self-sacrificial love.

Love is a paradoxical thing. It is an almighty helplessness and a non-forceful force. It is the meaning behind Jesus's saying that those who cling to their lives will lose them while those who lose their lives for the sake the kingdom will find them. It is the strange law by which those who sacrifice their happiness for others are the happiest of all. It is the paradox God himself proved when he conquered evil by dying on a cross. The living God died so that mortals, dead in their sins, would live.

God calls his people to live out this paradox in daily life. If we are Christ's disciples, we will deny ourselves, take up our cross, and follow him. This turns out not to be a solemn death march, however, but a joyful pilgrimage to the new Jerusalem, where Christ is already enthroned as king and where we will reign with him forever. But life along the road is difficult. To deny ourselves, although it is the path of life, goes against the grain of this world. We are called to deny the love of power and to embrace the power of love.

That is where we begin to see the scandal of love. Everybody likes the idea of love, but Jesus's command to love our enemies and pray for our persecutors seems outrageous to us. We crucify the command with a thousand qualifications: "Surely he didn't really mean for us to live this way.

It was a creative hyperbole. He only meant it for his twelve disciples. He meant it for the coming eschatological kingdom, not our life in this present world." But what if we really take Jesus absolutely seriously on this point? What if we see our mission in the world as something to be accomplished by the power of self-sacrificial love, rather than the power games by which the world normally gets things done? No doubt Christians will arrive at different practical answers to this specific question, but it is a question we cannot ignore.

Love and Holiness

It may be fair to say that ours is the age of the glorification of love. We are especially preoccupied with romantic and erotic love, but love in general is often held up as the solution to all our problems and as the ultimate human good. The problem with this is not so much that it is false (it seems that Christianity would ultimately, in a sense, agree with this), but that love is so frequently oversimplified and misunderstood. Too often the word means little more than being nice. People think they have loved when they have made someone feel good. It may be true that people who are loving want others to feel good, all other things being equal. And simple kindness to others surely is an important component of love. But the reality we encounter in Scripture—and in the character and actions of God—is something much greater. So much greater, in fact, that even understanding love is something that exceeds our natural capacities. This is why Ephesians 3 implies that we need God's power just to grasp the love of Christ. It even tells us, paradoxically, that by his power we are enabled to know the love that surpasses knowledge—that is, to know the unknowable.

What does it mean to know the unknowable? In this case, at least two things. First, it means knowing something by revelation from God which we could not have known on our own. God's love surpasses knowledge because it is a reality which exists above and beyond us. It is a reality of which we would know nothing apart from God's gracious choice to share it with us. God's love is not like a scientific discovery or a math equation which we can solve. In that case, it would be something that we could take as a given; something that, with clear thinking, is a rationally obvious fact about the universe. But when we see God's love, as we do most clearly on the cross, our reaction cannot be "Well of course!" God's love is the great surprise;

the great mystery and scandal whereby he gives himself sacrificially for the lowly and the undeserving.

Secondly, knowing the unknowable implies an experiential, participatory kind of knowledge. God's love is not something which can be adequately encompassed by our rational understanding. This does not mean that it is irrational; just that our rationality cannot fully comprehend it. Love is not merely an idea which is grasped by the mind, but also a reality which is enacted and experienced between persons. We do not know God's love when we have read enough theology textbooks, but when we have stood in awestruck wonder at the foot of the cross. After all, we do not know anything in the complete sense until we participate in it personally. God's love is not an abstract fact, but the living reality of the Trinity which he has invited us to enjoy, by his grace alone.

In short, to know God's love which is beyond all knowledge means knowing a reality which is infinitely beyond us, and yet one which has reached down to touch us and draw us in by sheer grace. It is here that we see the paradox of God's love and his holiness. Love is the reality of God; of the eternal Trinity. Love is therefore the ultimate reality. But in saying this, we are also saying that God's love, far from being a warm and cozy feeling of acceptance, is something absolutely *other*. Another word for that is *holy*.

Holiness is a word often used to describe God's perfect moral purity. But the central idea of holiness, from which that moral sense derives, is God's absolute purity of *being*: God is set-apart, in a class by himself, and nothing else is like him. To know that God is holy means knowing that he is infinitely greater than us. It means knowing that he is unknowable. The wonderful thing, though, is that the unknowable God wants us to know him and has introduced himself to us. God's *otherness* is an *otherness* which, paradoxically, reaches out to embrace us.[1]

There's another way we can put this. God's holiness means that he is absolutely and perfectly himself. This was hinted at when God introduced himself to Moses as "I Am That I Am." God is perfectly himself for all eternity through the reciprocal relation of the Trinity. But God, as the generous creator, is also absolutely committed to being himself in all his relations to the created world, in perfect faithfulness. That perhaps gets to the heart of the idea of *covenant* which is so important in the scriptural story of God's relationship with his people, and here we are reminded again of God's love.[2]

---

1. McCullough, *Trivialization of God*, 81–87.
2. This idea of God's love for his people and his world as an expression of his

Seen in this light, we are able to put God's holiness and love together. They are both grounded in the reality that God is absolutely committed to being himself in all his relations—to himself and to us. The ultimate reality of God's love is that which God has in himself in the relations of the trinitarian communion. That is also the ground of God's holiness: God is eternally bound to be true to himself. But God's holiness and his love, so conceived as realities within the Trinity, both spill over generously toward his created world. Therefore, God's love is holy because it is rooted in the ultimate reality of the Trinity which lies so far beyond us, and God's holiness is loving because he desires to share it with the world so that we might know him, and become more fully formed after his own image.

Let's look it from yet another angle. Ephesians 3 makes the wonderful statement that we are rooted and grounded in God's love. In other words, love is the reality in which we live as God's people. This is reflected in the great commandments to love God and to love our neighbors. That is the heart of what God wants of us. When we love, we are responding appropriately to what God has done for us, and in fact, to who God is. The apostle John tells us repeatedly that "God is Love." To love is to sing the same tune as ultimate reality. Remember that the very creation of the world, besides being an act of power, was an act of love. Therefore, reality itself is surrounded by love, even as all of history is surrounded by God's eternal purpose. This is why Paul can describe Christ's love with the language of infinite physical dimensions: it is unfathomably high and deep, long and wide. The Christian is the person who lives in joyful obedience to this fact. Those who persist in rebellion will eventually find themselves outsiders to a universe filled with God's love.

This language which describes God's love—high, deep, long, and wide—tells us of its unfathomable greatness. But as it does so, it forces us to look beyond ourselves.[3] That is almost the definition of love, so this should

---

commitment to be perfectly himself in all his relations is elegantly conveyed in 2 Tim 2:13, in which Paul says, quoting a saying, "if we are faithless, he remains faithful, for he cannot disown himself"

3. We see here that love and holiness, different as they appear to us at first glance, are actually conceptually united in the idea of looking beyond ourselves. Wherever there is authentic love, there is an element of transcendence; of knowing and touching something or someone that is *not me*. Such transcendence, when it is referring to the difference between humans and God, is the meaning of the word *holiness*. Holy transcendence is the precondition for loving union. Authentic relations between persons require both a differentiation, or a set-apartness, and a loving desire to overcome that difference through interpersonal discourse. This dynamic is present to some degree in all human

not surprise us. Yet we are surprised. It is our habit, as self-centered people, to think of God's love as though it were all about us. We think that the phrase "God is absolutely loving" must equate to "God accepts me just the way I am," or "I should feel perfectly comfortable." It is amazing how we can leap from "God is love" to "Aren't we such great people?" We think of God's love as a fact about ourselves, when it is a fact about God. God is love, and he was love before the universe (let alone humans) ever existed. God, as Trinity, has always been a communion of perfect love; an eternal dance of self-emptying delight. It is here, not in our human-centered (or perhaps just self-centered) feelings, that we come to understand what love really is. God's love is an eternal reality—*the* eternal reality. To know God's love is the closest we can come to gazing into the depths of the Divine Being. But God's love, as such, is not about us. It is about him. It is a reality of his own glory in which, by his sheer grace, we are invited to participate.

We see here again how God's love and his holiness are interpenetrating. His love is absolute; a reality of his divine perfection. It is therefore holy, and indeed cannot be understood apart from his holiness. But God's holiness—his royal majesty, perfect goodness, supreme otherness—has been made known to us by his loving grace. Therefore, the question of whether God's love or his holiness is greater turns out to be an unanswerable one. God is absolutely loving, but the reality of his love, like the reality of his very being, is infinitely beyond us and therefore infinitely holy. On the other hand, the reason we can even know that God is holy—or that he exists at all—is because he has stooped to reveal himself to us; because he is interested enough in us to create us in the first place, to make us capable of knowing him, and to seek us out when we lost our way. In other words, we know that he is holy only because he loves us so much that he wants us to know him. Comparing God's holiness and his love, then, is like comparing the height of his throne to the length of his arm. We cannot say that one is greater than the other because both are infinite. In fact, they define each other. God's love for us is precisely that which spans the infinite distance between him and us. We know the greatness of God's love because of the size of the gulf it has crossed. We know the greatness of God's holiness because we have seen the magnitude of love which was required to satisfy it; namely, the cross.

---

relationships, but is most completely reflected in the God-human relationship. It is also present in the Trinity, which includes both difference between persons and union of being.

Perhaps this is all rather cerebral. What does this really mean for us? On the one hand, it means that we can and should unreservedly assert the greatness of God's love for us. We don't need to tip-toe around that truth or qualify it with hesitant disclaimers in fear of offending God's holiness. We are finite beings with finite concepts of love. No matter how big our idea of love is, God's love must be bigger. God's holiness and love are not in competition with each other. They are both perfect. They are like two lines which might begin far apart in our human vantage point, but which converge to a single point in the heart of God. That is a place far beyond our sight—unless, that is, we are looking at the cross. Only then can we confidently say that "God is love," and that his relationship to you and me and the whole world is ultimately defined by this reality.

At the same time, many popular notions of God's love must be challenged, especially those which try to understand God's love apart from his holiness. There is an unspoken assumption that is frequently implied when people say that "God is love," which is that God must conform to our own (rather watered-down) idea of love. It becomes permission for us to reject any description of God or action attributed to him which makes us uncomfortable. As modern people, we tend to assume that if God is absolutely loving, he will never exercise wrath against sin. We assume that love involves looking the other way when it comes to matters of justice and punishment. But this is clearly not what God's love means, if God's self-presentation gets to define love. God's love is inseparable from his absolute commitment to perfect goodness. If we think about it long at all, we realize that the indifference to right and wrong implied in the contemporary attraction to non-judgmentalism actually makes real love impossible. Real love, defined as a self-giving commitment to the good of the other, can only exist in a framework in which good and evil, righteousness and sin, are taken absolutely seriously. God did not enact his love by denying his absolute opposition to our sin. That would have been a defect of God's goodness, which is the only basis on which our own good (or any good) is a meaningful concept. God enacted his love by realizing his opposition to sin in an incomprehensible self-sacrifice.

Therefore, when we say that God is absolutely loving, this does not allow us pin God down into our corner. It is not a principle by which we can fully understand God and predict all his behaviors. God is never less than loving. But God's love seems to be something far bigger and wilder than we tend to suppose. God's love surrounds us like a flood and drowns out all fear. And yet it is not a gentle, harmless benevolence. It is a consuming fire. It is the infinite self-giving and self-commitment of the Trinity expressed in perfect faithfulness to himself and to all reality. God's love, as utmost reality, is a sharp-edged thing. It is the scalpel by which he cuts the sin from the sinner like cancer from flesh. It is the sword of his eternal victory on which he himself has fallen to save us all. God's love, after all, has no other name than the cross.

Like we have said, it is our tendency as self-centered beings to interpret God's love for us as an occasion for admiring ourselves, when it ought to inspire a self-forgetful admiration of God. God's love is not a fact about us, but rather a fact about God.

However, there is an important qualification to this; a sense in which God does loves us because of something we are. Not, of course, because of anything we have done or any kind of moral excellence we possess, but because of something which we cannot help being: God's creation, made in his image. God loves us because he made us. God makes what he loves and loves what he makes. Otherwise he wouldn't have made it. God loves us not for what we have made of ourselves, but for what he has made us to be, and what he desires to redeem in us.

Here we see that God's act of creation is a paradoxical contact point between himself and humanity. It is paradoxical because the very act by which God touches the world also sets him infinitely apart from it. The difference between creator and creation is absolute, but it is also the basis for the relationship between the two. Both sides of this paradox inform our theology of God's love. God is the infinite *other* who loves only because of who he is; and yet at the same time, God's love freely spills over into his creation, coloring it with his glory, and motivating his commitment to redeem the good things he has made.[4]

What this means for us is that in the one sense, God's love is a fact about God, not us. It calls us to admire him, not ourselves. And yet in another sense, God's love is that which has created us and redeemed us, and it defines us for all eternity. God's love is then a fact about God which by his grace has become—and still is becoming—a fact about us. That is the heart of the *mystery* which Paul celebrates in Ephesians: God's eternal purpose to create a people to bear his image, to recreate them after the pattern of Jesus Christ, and in this way to draw them into the trinitarian fellowship of love for all eternity. The most important thing about each of us—and our

---

4. Peckham, *Love of God*, 98–100.

human race collectively—is that we are loved by God as his creatures and as participants in his great drama of redemption.

Love and Glory

Paul closes his prayer for knowledge of God's unfathomable love with a stirring doxology: an exclamation of God's glory. He says: "To him be glory forever and ever, through his holy people in Christ Jesus for all generations. Amen." In doing so, he has fastened together two of the most powerful themes of the Christian faith: God's love and God's glory. We feel a sense of theological tension between these two themes, as we did between God's love and his holiness. It is, in fact, a tension which plays out in many historical and current theological discussions, and it is visible in the way different Christians have answered this question: does God ultimately act on behalf of his glory, or his love?

Soli Deo Gloria (glory to God alone) was one of the rallying cries of the Reformation, and it is the rightful focus of all Christian belief and living. Our ultimate desire in life should be to glorify God. Many theologians have emphasized how God's own ultimate purpose for all that he has done is to magnify his own glory. But this also raises troubling questions, namely: is God ultimately selfish? Does he merely want to use people for their worship? Is God a megalomaniac with a pathological need to be the center of attention? If so, what does that do our conviction that God is love?

This problem is resolved by thinking more carefully about the meaning of God's glory. We often talk as though glory is something which we can give and which God can receive. In one sense, this is true. The word *glory* has a wide range of meaning in its biblical usages, and one meaning is the idea of fame, reputation, or being known. We can give God glory in this sense of giving him our worshipful recognition. But when we know God and revere him for who he is, we are not adding something to God or giving him something he needs. There is a sense in which we can give nothing to God. He already has everything. Glory, in the sense of fame, involves the recognition on our part of that which God already is. God's glory in itself never increases; rather it increases in and among us as we come to know and celebrate who he is. When we do this, who really benefits? We do. God was absolutely complete before he created the world or its inhabitants. God doesn't need our worship. Worship is the gift in which God gives us the opportunity to delight in him as we come to know him. We are the ones who need worship. It is the creation, not the Creator, which is incomplete without it. We glorify God by coming to know him for who he is, calling others to know him, and rejoicing together in that knowledge. The fact that God earnestly desires our worship and delights in it is therefore a testament to his loving care for us and his relational desire to draw us to himself.

The word *glory* can also be used to collectively signify all those attributes for which God is rightly praised, such as his goodness, wisdom, power, and love. Again, to glorify God cannot mean adding anything to these, but only responding to them in worship. But these attributes can be increasingly manifested in the world. In fact, one good definition for the glory of God could be *God's goodness made visible and manifest in the world*. God in himself is perfectly holy, wise, and loving. His desire is for the whole world, and in particular his own people, to reflect and share in his holiness, wisdom, and love.

If we return to our question as to whether God ultimately acts on behalf of his glory or his love, it should now be clear that this is a false dichotomy. God's glory includes his love. Not only that, but the very fact that God acts for his glory in the universe has its basis in his love. God, as ultimate reality, is the one single source of all goodness. His desire to glorify himself simply means that he doesn't want to keep his goodness to himself but to share it with his whole created universe for all to enjoy. God's glory is fundamentally generous, not selfish.[5]

Unfortunately, we sometimes have the tendency to speak as though God were like a cosmic celebrity addicted to the glamour of the spotlight. Austin Fischer suggests a very helpful image to describe this misconception: some people think of God as a black hole, eternally pulling everything else into himself.[6] We find a better astronomical analogy for God in a huge, brilliant star, expelling glorious light and energy outward in every direction. Like a black hole, the star is incredibly massive and exerts a

---

5. When we ask the question whether God is selfish, we also need to remember the Trinity. God is not a solitary person, but a tri-personal being. This gives a new flavor to the reality that God is God-centered. His God-centeredness does not take the form of egocentricity, but interpersonal love, which spills over into all his interpersonal relations.

6. Fischer, *Young, Restless, No Longer Reformed*. I personally agree with Fischer's argument against Calvinism. However, I am not sure he is fair in suggesting that Calvinists have an idea of God which can be compared to a black hole. My experience suggests to me that most Calvinists would agree with the picture of God as radiantly generous rather than needy and greedy. The problem lies not with Calvinism, but with certain careless ways of talking and thinking about God's glory which (usually unintentionally) portray God this way.

tremendous gravitational pull, but in this case its gravity serves to draw countless planets into its orbit, illuminating and warming them through its rays and turning each into a small reflection of its splendor. God's glory is something he desires to share with us.[7] He wants us to bask in it, as we rejoice in who he is, and consequently, in who he has made us to be. That is the opposite of selfish. God does not crave the spotlight. He *is* the spotlight, and he intends to light up the whole universe.

This perspective on God's glory also clears up a few other misunderstandings. One is the idea that there is always a zero-sum equation between God's glory and human glory. We can take it as foundational that any glory which a created thing enjoys comes in the first place from the creator. There can be no real competition between God and humans in this sense. Whatever goodness, beauty, or excellence we possess is purely a gift from God. Of course, this is precisely why we must insist on giving God all the glory rather than claiming some for ourselves, if by glory we mean credit, merit, or inherent worthiness. It is ridiculous to think that any of this is something we deserve or have manufactured on our own. But God is not anxious that we will steal his glory, if by glory we mean his revealed and manifested goodness. If anything, we want his glory too little. I expect that he means to give us far more of it than we, in our present state, can handle.

Similarly, we should not be concerned that belief in human agency and free will is a threat to God's glory. If, for example, there is a role for human agency in responding freely to God's offer of salvation (and I believe that there is), that does not detract from God's glory. If anything, it enhances it further. I believe that God chose to manifest his glory in the universe precisely by endowing some of his creatures with freedom and personhood. This freedom allows for relational realities such as love, trust,

---

7. The idea of God sharing his glory may raise some red flags as we recall the statement which God makes in Isaiah 48:11, "For my own sake, for my own sake I do this. How can I let myself be defamed? I will not yield my glory to another." However, the context of this statement is Israel's idolatry. God is incomparably greater than these false objects of worship. God does not yield his glory to another in the sense that he will not tolerate any rivals to the claim of divinity. God will not allow the deception whereby people call things "gods" which are not God. Again, it is God's people, and not God himself, who will come to harm if they succumb to this deception. The fact that God seems to take it personally and is concerned about this "for my own sake" is actually a profound statement of his love. God is hurt and angered by the outrage of idolatry because he cares enough for his people to be emotionally invested in their ultimate wellbeing. This is an example of what we have said above about God's holy love as an absolute commitment to being himself in all his relations.

and obedience—aspects of God's glorious character which he desires to put on display in us, and in the relationship between himself and his people. When a creature makes a non-determined choice, this does not invade the sphere of God's sovereignty and diminish his greatness. It points to his greatness by exhibiting his sovereign choice to make the kind of a world in which these beautiful relational realities can unfold, all to the praise of his infinite wisdom and goodness. When a person freely responds to God's gracious initiative—or even if she refuses—she is displaying the glory of God in a way that a world of meticulous determinism never could.

Finally, something should be said about the relationship between God's glory and his wrath. It is true that God's wrath is an expression of his glory. It is an expression of his holiness, and even of his love, if our definition of his love includes his absolute trinitarian commitment to be true to his own goodness. But God's wrath is not an *inherently necessary* expression of his glory. Wrath is not one of God's essential attributes. It is an effect of his attribute of perfect goodness, when it encounters evil. This is contrary to certain arguments for double predestination, in which God planned out a hell filled with people before the creation of all worlds just to allow for a proper display of his wrath. This would mean that it is part of God's essential nature to be angry and that he created certain things just so that he could be angry against them. In fact, God's anger against sin is very real and very serious. But this is precisely because sin is the rebellion of free creatures against his goodness. His wrath therefore displays his glory with respect to a fallen world, but not in such a way that the fall itself was necessary for this purpose.

Conclusion: The Call to Worship

Just as we saw in our exploration of God's love in relation to his power and his holiness, God's love and his glory are not in competition with one another. The closer we get to these realities, the more we see them merge together into the singular perfection of the Trinity. Specifically, God's glory—that is, his perfect goodness made visible for us to know and enjoy—is an expression of his self-giving love. Conversely, God's self-sacrificial love is one of the most striking expressions of his glory. We are awed before the grandeur and majesty of God in his omnipotence. But when we see how the almighty king of the universe humbly laid down his life for his disloyal subjects, our awe crosses an entirely new and higher threshold of amazement.

The clear response to all this is worship. We desire to join our voices with Paul and the Ephesian church as we sing the praise of God's glory. That is a fundamental task of the church. We as God's people have been redeemed to our creation-calling of knowing that the Lord is God and enacting that knowledge in all our activities and relationships. We are called to be the community of *doxology*: the proclamation and celebration of God's glory.

It so happens that such worship is something our world desperately needs. This is not because worship is something people have forgotten how to do. The truth is that everybody worships. Humans cannot help but worship something, even when there appears to be nothing worth worshipping. In that case, we will worship something worthless. The human heart cannot abide a worship vacuum.

That raises the question of what happens when people turn their worship to a wrong object, to something in creation rather than the creator, to the work of our own hands (or heads), to our nation or empire, or (and maybe this gets to the heart of it all) our own selves. The situation is particularly acute in a secular civilization such as ours, in which it often seems that there is no love that lasts forever, nothing to thank for beauty and happiness but our own neurons, nothing to praise but our own accomplishments, and nothing to hope for but what we can contrive out of our circumstances. The human heart was created to delight in God; without him, there is despair.

The church is the embodiment of God's answer to this problem. We are meant to be the community of those who, through the grace of Jesus Christ, remember our primordial human calling to worship God. Seen this way, the church is not a strange sect living on the lonely margins of the world (however we may be regarded in the current order of things), but rather stands, being gathered around the cross, at the center of all things. We are those who have gathered around the crucified and risen Christ to revere him and follow him into the new creation, in which creation's original purpose of worship is restored.

We see then how worship and love merge together. When we see how we have been loved by God, our response is to love him in return, and to express this love by loving our neighbors, partnering with God in his mission of manifesting his goodness and love in the world. In doing so, we help make his glory visible, as we participate in it and enjoy it together. As bearers of the divine image, this is our love for God, and God's love for the world put to work in and through us.

The Scandal of Love

Through Christ, God has loved us outrageously; scandalously. In doing so, he has glorified himself and invited us to enjoy that glory with him forever. We are therefore called, in the here and now, to live out an existence marked by love and worship. It is an existence which scandalizes the world. We see this scandal in our paradoxical calling to love the world precisely by being set apart from it. We are called to serve the world with self-sacrificial love, but never merely for its sake or on its terms, for we are called to give our worship and allegiance to God alone.

This scandalous existence, grounded in our identity as a human people graciously set apart by God's love for his glorious purposes in Christ, is the matter which occupies the second half of the book of Ephesians. God has told us who, and what, we are. He has shown us the meaning of all things and our relation as redeemed sinners to that great meaning. But what does it mean really to live that out; both socially as God's holy people, and as individuals responsible before God? To these questions we turn our attention.

Lord, when we consider the ungraspable beauty of who you are—which we know we cannot even truly imagine—we can only stand in awe. Thank you for who you are. Thank you for being who you are to us! Thank you for letting us know and benefit from who you are. Lord, we want to keep on knowing who you are; and not merely knowing, but responding to who you are in our daily activities and habits of the heart. Make us a people whose life is worship; a celebration of your great love. May your greatness be lived in us. Help us to follow you Lord, to affirm you by denying ourselves, for your sake, for your church, for your world, and your eternal glory in Christ Jesus. Amen.

7

The Scandal of the Church

Paraphrase: Ephesians 4:1-16

AS A CAPTIVE TO *Christ's calling, therefore, I urge you to lead a life worthy of this calling. Such a life is marked by humility, gentleness, patience, and bearing with one another in love. Make every effort to protect and nurture the unity which you have together in the Holy Spirit, which is your bond of peace. For this is what you are: one body through one Spirit, one calling to one hope, one faith and one baptism into one Lord, before the one God and father of all, who is above all, through all, and in all.*

However, we have each received Christ's gracious gifts uniquely. This is why it is said: "When he ascended on high, he took many captives, and gave gifts to his people." (That "He ascended" must mean that he had also descended into the lower reaches of earth. The one who descended here to us has also ascended far above the heavens, so as to fulfill all things). These gifts include the callings he gave to different people to be apostles, prophets, evangelists, pastors, and teachers. Their work (God's gift) is to equip God's holy people for service, so that the body of Christ will be built up. And this is what God is building toward: our unity in faith and knowledge of his son, and our maturity, so that we might be fully grown-up as the body of Christ. So we cannot remain childlike and immature, tossed back and forth on the waves; blown adrift on the stormy sea of the world's empty beliefs and the wiles of false teachers. Instead, as we speak the truth in love, we must grow up into Christ, who is our source and goal. In him the whole body is joined together, with all its tendons, ligaments, and tissues working in harmony. In this way, the body develops and thrives, as it is built up in love.

The Scandal of the Church

God created humanity to be his holy people—his own special possession. In our God-given freedom (a necessary prerequisite for this calling), we have all gone astray. God's work of redemption has therefore involved calling one particular people (the Jews) to demonstrate his solution to this problem: a covenantal relationship between God and people; that is, a transformative relationship founded on the basis of God's loving promises. But not even these people could truly embody the faithful purposes of God, for they too went astray, as have we all. God's ultimate solution is to create a new reality through the death and resurrection of Jesus Christ. In him, God has succeeded in fulfilling the human task on our behalf, but in such a way as to invite us into this fulfillment so that we may truly live it out before the watching world. This redeemed-and-redeeming community of people is called the church.

Ephesians chapter 4 is rooted in these truths. In the first half of this letter, Paul has unveiled the *mystery*: that Jesus Christ is the meaning and fulfillment of all things, and that we, a human people who live by faith, are participants in that fulfillment. This is the way in which the meaning of the universe becomes the meaning of our lives. We have been told who and what we are. But now Paul begins to unpack what it means to inhabit this truth in daily life.

One of the great habitual mistakes of human philosophy has been to conceive of truth merely as an idea which is known and not also as a life to be lived and a task to be accomplished (and Christianly speaking, as a person to be trusted). It is true that philosophy at its best has not made this mistake. Most of the great philosophers have been intensely interested in connecting the question "what is truth?" to the question "how should we live?" It may be the case that these are, in fact, simply different sides of the same question. To neglect either one is actually to misunderstand the other. Still, much philosophy and also theology have lost sight of this. It has been forgotten that the purpose of our knowledge of reality is the cultivation of a right relationship with it in the context of our human lives. To invoke philosophical language, there has sometimes been a tendency to be concerned about *being* (ultimate, timeless reality) at the expense of *existence* (reality as it is experienced and lived in the here-and-now). On the other hand, the opposite error is just as dangerous, in which we think that our present, earthly existence which we experience is all that there is. We forget that it has its basis in the eternal purposes of God. To forget either side of reality is to fundamentally misunderstand the whole. The old debate about whether we should be heavenly-minded or more concerned about the earthly good is therefore a false dichotomy of the highest order. We cannot share the mind of heaven without being concerned about his purposes for our life on earth. Conversely, we cannot really comprehend the meaning of the earthly good apart from its basis in the eternal purposes and character of God.

All of this is simply to say that God's great purpose for us is not merely a nice idea. He really means for us to live it out in the world today. *"The people of God"* is not just a conceptual scheme; it is a real society of flesh-and-blood human persons. We cannot get around this: the church, as a fellowship of human persons who are united to Christ through faith, is the embodiment of God's purposes for humanity.

Maturity through Unity and Diversity

The message of Ephesians 4:1–16 concerning the church can be summarized in three words: unity, diversity, and maturity. Paul describes the church repeatedly as something that is growing; more specifically growing up to so as to fully realize its identity as the body of Christ. Therefore, that the church is the embodiment of Christ in the world is true in an already-but-not-yet sense. Because the church only exists in the first place through the union with Christ which believers collectively enjoy, the church cannot help but be the body of Christ. Yet Paul also describes this as a work-in-progress. He instructs the Ephesians to continue to grow toward realizing this identity in its maturity. This is accomplished through the marriage of unity and diversity. Paul urges his audience to realize their essential unity as members in the singular reality of God's purposes enacted through Jesus Christ. This is a unity which, as we saw in 2:11–22, tears down all human hostilities and divisions by creating a new and greater circle of solidary which dethrones the exclusive claims of old allegiances. But this unity in no way involves uniformity. God's singular purpose is enacted through a great variety of gifts and offices. God's new-creation project is not like a factory assembly line, but more like a garden, or even a zoo (readers of Genesis will not be surprised). Everything, by being uniquely itself, contributes to the life and beauty of the whole ecosystem.

We should not think for a moment that in this chapter, Paul has moved on from matters of theological and philosophical significance so as to address the pragmatics of the life of the church. As we suggested above, this very dichotomy is probably a false one. Here we need to notice the great theological and philosophical import which are contained in the words *maturity, unity,* and *diversity.*

Maturity

The word *maturity*, especially as it is used in this passage, indicates a process of growth toward a goal or a state of completion. It's a concept which is implied in many of Jesus' parables about kingdom growth, in which he uses a seed as one of his main analogies. The kingdom of God is compared to seeds which are scattered on the ground and mysteriously grow into a crop of grain (Mark 4:26–29). It is also compared to a mustard seed which starts out very small, but grows into a garden shrub large enough for birds to perch on its branches (Luke 13:18–19). Jesus also tells a story in which a farmer casts seeds upon the ground, where they face various impediments to growth, but in which the final result is a crop springing up from the good soil which reproduces a hundredfold what was scattered (Luke 8:1–15). There is a conceptual kinship between the main idea in these parables and the kind of growth toward maturity which Paul discusses in Ephesians 4. It the same is idea conveyed in Philippians 1:6, in which Paul says that he is confident that "he who began a good work in you will carry it on to completion until the day of Christ Jesus." It is the kind of completion in which a thing is growing toward the actualization of that which it already is. That is the nature of the development of a seed. The seed is the carrier of genetic material which determines what it will become. Similarly, the Christian life, both individually and corporately, is a process of becoming that which we already are. This is an idea to which we will return in the next chapter as well.

There is a strong resonance here with some ideas of Aristotle which have been very influential throughout history, especially in relation to the philosophical theology of Thomas Aquinas in the middle ages. Aristotle described change and motion in terms of *potentiality* and *actuality*. Actuality, for Aristotle, is a state of perfection in which the essence of a thing is actualized. This is, for example, how he conceived of human happiness, or *eudemonia*. He described it as the full realization of the human ethical good. By the perfecting of the virtues essential to our human good (such as justice, courage, self-control, and moderation), we should, in theory, achieve a state of actualization where all is as it should be and there is nothing more to be desired. This basic idea has been applied by Christians such as Augustine and Thomas Aquinas through a more theologically informed view of life, in which the greatest good is not earthly human virtue but eternal knowledge and enjoyment of God.

However, there are a few more important distinctions we should make between this Aristotelian view of maturation/self-realization and what biblically-informed theology should assert. For Aristotle, this kind of development was inherent in nature. We certainly do see this in nature; for example, in a seed. But Christians are living according to the supernatural reality of God's gracious redemption, not according to our nature in which we were born. This redemption is not the development of our best inner self which we have always possessed, but is the gift of new life given by God through Jesus Christ and the Holy Spirit. We are not transformed by our own inner resources and potentialities, but by the grace of God. According to Ephesians 4, the end goal of this process of maturation is not our achievement of individual self-actualization, but that we, together as God's people, will grow up into the embodiment of Jesus Christ. In one sense, this is in fact a process of self-actualization. By God's grace, we are becoming the people which he created us to be in the first place, and which we are now recreated to be, with Jesus Christ as both the source and the goal of this transformation.

This turns many popular notions of self-actualization on their head. In the context of human sin and fallenness, becoming our true selves, in the most real sense, involves dying to the myriad "selves" we create to affirm our own significance, and putting on the "self" which is defined by Jesus Christ and which is formed collectively by God's people.[1] The irony of this, however, is that our true selfhood is in no way squelched: here alone is our true God-given identity and individuality realized. True freedom is found in becoming that which God created us to be. It is that which we were according to creation, which we have lost according to the fall, which we are again according to our union with Jesus Christ, and which we are learning to become in our inner attitudes and patterns of daily life together. It is the image of God in us, which we have always possessed simply by being God's human creatures, but which we have failed to reflect as God intended. God

---

1. This forms a contrast with attempts to inform our sense of self either individualistically according to our own desires and inclinations, or socially through memberships in circles of solidarity which claim supremacy. As was discussed in chapter 4, this is the contrast between egocentricity and ethnocentricity, which amount to different forms of the same basic condition.

has restored us as his image-bearers by presenting his perfect image-bearer, Jesus Christ, into whose image and likeness we are being formed together as God's holy people. Only by turning our faces away from ourselves and toward the brilliance of God's glory which is manifest in Jesus Christ are we illuminated; illuminated to reveal not only who God is, but who in fact we are. Our collective conformity to the image of Jesus Christ brings out rather than diminishes our individual uniqueness. The manifold glory of God can only be reflected by the almost infinite variety which exists among his people.

Unity and Diversity

Now we have begun to see the relationship between unity and diversity as they contribute toward the completion of God's people as the embodiment of Jesus Christ. The maturity of God's people is not brought about by a slavish uniformity, nor by a narcissistic individualism, but by the many unique manifestations of God's gracious gift working together in harmony of purpose. This marriage of unity and diversity is on one level a very practical way of approaching the challenges of shared life together in a community. It is one of the hallmarks of excellence in all kinds of corporate endeavors. We think about great human accomplishments, such as NASA's moon missions. This required the union of many diverse gifts: thousands upon thousands of immensely talented individuals working together harmoniously on a common purpose. We also think of a symphony orchestra, whose excellence requires not only many masterful musicians, but an ability to play their different instruments together as one musical force. When encountering any organizational problem, we can find clarity by observing and addressing these two factors (individual abilities and collective purpose) and the state of their relationship to one another.

But when we think about this marriage of unity and diversity, we are not just regarding a practicality of organizational life. We are pondering something close to the heart of reality itself. We are in fact wrestling once again with the great philosophical question of the one and the many. This is a question of both intellectual and practical concern. We wonder how the universe, in all its great diversity, coheres together in a single, unified rationality. It is of practical concern because so much in our world seems broken and fragmented, and we long for it to be put back together again.

A Scandalous People

We saw in chapter 1 that the Christian answer to this question/problem is the person of Jesus Christ. It is in him, as creator and redeemer, that reality coheres and that our seemingly chaotic world is drawn toward a destiny defined by the glory and love of God. But as we have also seen in our study of Ephesians, the victory of Jesus Christ is not merely a fact hanging from on high: it is a reality in which human beings are called to participate through union with Christ by faith. This then is the implication of belonging to the body of Christ: it means living at the juncture of the one and the many. It means living in our different situations with our different gifts and identities, for the singular purpose of God which is defined through Jesus Christ.

To be a Christian therefore involves living contrary to certain worldly philosophies. As Paul says, we refuse to be blown about by the wind and waves of the world's teachings. Some philosophies stress the one at the expense of the many. This is characteristic of many Eastern worldviews, in addition to certain strains of Greek philosophy. In this case, the world of our experiences and our bodily, relational lives, which are marked by so many important distinctions, are seen as illusory. The only ultimate reality according to this perspective is that all is one. The one swallows the many and dissolves them into the ocean of Nirvana or the absolute. On the other hand, there are some more contemporary philosophies which stress the many at the expense of the one. This is characteristic of postmodernism, which sees reality as fragmented to the degree that we should not even try to see all of life in light of a single coherent scheme. For example, according to this perspective, there is no such thing as history; only the various stories told by different communities. Rather than an ocean which absorbs all diverse identities and experiences, here those identities and experiences are ultimately atomized into a billion separate universes.

The Christian worldview lives between these two extremes. Reality has a central focal point, which is the trinitarian God who has revealed himself and redeemed the world in the person of Jesus Christ. Because there is one God, there is one single ultimate origin of all things and one single rightful allegiance of all creatures. There is a single destiny and goal for all things in the glorification of God. But it has never been God's purpose to absorb all things into himself. The glory of God is achieved in his manifold wisdom whereby all created things display his goodness in and through their own uniqueness. Every person is made to display the same image of God, but

The Scandal of the Church

each with their own particular tint. God's choir sings in harmony, but not in unison.

God has destined us for union with him and with one another, but it is the kind of union which presupposes and requires our distinction from him and one another. That is the foundational relational reality which is rooted in the Trinity itself. God, as three persons in one being, is a unity and a diversity at the same time. This relational dynamic actually underlies all life in our experience. A relationship between two people requires a contact or connection between them, but without compromising their distinct identities. Otherwise, they would not be two people in a relationship, but in fact a single person. This sense of union-with-distinctness is required even to know anything about the world around us. We can understand something about our own universe because we live in union or connection with it as participants, yet in distinction from it as rational observers. For example, we can only study a newly discovered species because we live in the same physical world with it and therefore can interact with it through the laws of nature by which we all live, but also only because we stand far enough over it to have at least somewhat of an objective point of view. All of life exists in this kind of dance between the diversity of things in their uniqueness and the vast web of interconnection by which nothing exists on its own. From this point of view, the one-and-the-many turns out not to be a problem at all, but the heartbeat of reality; the rhythm of the trinitarian dance pulsating joyously through the whole universe.[2]

But above all, this reality of unity-and-diversity is reflected in the community of God's redeemed image-bearers: the Church. We as individuals are created in God's image, but we cannot fully carry out our task of displaying God's image on our own. We can only do it through our union with Christ, who as the God-man is the only perfectly successful image-bearer, and we can only do it together as God's redeemed community. That is what it means to be the body of Christ as the church. It means that against the current of false unities and false diversities which the world

---

2. We are also reminded here of our previous reflections on the relationship between God's holiness and his love in chapter 6. God's holiness refers to his absolute distinction from the world; his total "set-apart-ness." But God's love refers to the fact that God has embraced the world from which he is so distinctly set apart. The distinction between God and the world (which we connect to his holiness), is actually the precondition for the glorious union with it which he has predestined in his love. Here we see how the dynamic of the one and many, of union and distinction, plays out (as it does so many other places) in the relationship between God's love and his holiness.

offers in endless forms, we mirror the unity and diversity which is in God himself through our mature union with Christ together as the church. This reaffirms what was said in the previous chapter: that the great task of the church is the worship of God, in which his redeemed image-bearers gather to reflect, celebrate, and participate in his glory.

The Problem of the Church

We have now seen what a glorious reality the church is. As the body of Christ, it is a reenactment of the Trinity itself. It is the community which declares and embodies God's solution (Jesus Christ) for all that has gone wrong in the world. This is all well and good, until we remember that this is no mere theological idea: it is meant to be a reality that is lived and experienced here on earth. Then we are confronted with one of the most challenging questions which can be set before the Christian faith: why doesn't the church reliably accomplish this? Why doesn't it consistently live out the righteousness of God? Why does the church, by and large, suffer from the same moral and social problems as the rest of the world? Why is it that the church sometimes becomes a contributor to the world's problems of pride, hatred, and division, rather than an enactor of the solution?

For readers of Scripture, this is not a new problem at all. This is the problem which Israel faced repeatedly. They were meant to be the bearers of God's solution to the brokenness of the world, but throughout their history at many points, they became just as lost and broken as the world into which they were sent. To use a word-picture given by Jesus, it was a case of the blind leading the blind. The solution to which Israel ultimately pointed was Jesus Christ, and in that respect they were successful. But we as the church are meant to inhabit the finished work of Christ as we live in the world as his redeemed representatives. And yet, it seems like we are back into the same situation: the church which sings "I once was lost, but now am found" often seems to live as though it is still just as lost as everyone else. In light of what we have said about the church's role and identity (the vindication of God's wisdom, the embodiment of Christ in the world, participation in God's redemptive act of bringing all things together in Christ), the condition of the church may actually be a more significant challenge to the Christian faith than the problem of evil.

What can be said about this? This is a question which cannot be adequately addressed within the scope of this chapter, so what follows will simply be the listing of a few points which should be considered as we seek to articulate a response based on the vision of the church which we have encountered in Ephesians.

Don't Exaggerate the Problem

Although the ongoing sinfulness which is present in the church is undoubtably a serious problem, we should be cautious about exaggerating it or seeing it in a one-sided way. Perhaps all Christians have either experienced a major disappointment with the church or else have known someone who has. There are a great many people who have left the church altogether because of their painful experiences with it. While this is sobering, we should be aware of the tendency for this side of the story to capture our whole attention while we ignore all the good that has been done and is still being done in the church. The church certainly has had and still has major, sobering problems, but it has also gotten more than its fair share of negative press. Perhaps this has something to do with human nature. The stories and experiences which stick in our minds tend to be the negative ones. We see this tendency played out extravagantly in news reporting. It also distorts our image of the church. The failures of the church to live up to its mission and identity as the community of the redeemed and the representative of Christ may be many, but we should not be blind to its many successes, which too often fly under the radar of our attention.

We are reminded of the prophet Elijah, who despaired at the condition of Israel while Baal worship was in its heyday. But God reminded him that he had reserved seven thousand true Israelites who had not bowed to Baal. God really has a people; people who, while imperfect, are really living to worship him and love their neighbors. If we are willing to look beyond our own discouragement, we will probably quickly realize that we have known many such persons; "True Israelites in whom there is no deception." They may be fewer than we would desire, yet they are more common than we would have guessed, and God, in his grace, is always making more of them. When we ask God "Where are these faithful people?," we find God asking us in return, "Are you willing to become such a person yourself?"

We Need to Think Clearly about the True Mission of the Church

We sometimes believe that the church is a failure simply because there are still as many problems in the world as there are. We assume that if the church was "the real deal" then there would no longer be poverty, sickness, and war in the world. It may be true that if we were as faithful as we ought to be, there would be a good deal less of these things. But we should not assume that it is the church's job to eliminate all evil and suffering in the world. Our mission, despite what is often assumed, is not simply to make the world a better place. It is true that the faithfulness of God's people will in fact result in the world becoming a better place. But the essence of the church's mission is not to fix the world. It is to point the world to its savior, as we both declare and embody the gospel of God's redeeming love. The church's mission is to point toward the reality of the kingdom of God in which it already lives, and which will one day, by a power greater than our own, become fully manifest on earth. The church must indeed be held accountable for its failures to do this. But the church cannot be blamed for failure to turn earth into a paradise when this is something which no power can accomplish but God's own eschatological promise to create the new heavens and the new earth.

We Need to Think Clearly about the True Identity of the Church

Before we accuse the church of whole-scale failure, we also need to be clear about what the church actually is. Here we are forced to make a distinction between the church which God has created in Jesus Christ, and the church as it is founded by human beings. In a sense, then, we could say that there are two churches. The first is a fellowship; the second an institution. The first is created by God the Father through the Son and the Spirit; the second is created by human beings. The first is the cruciform body of Christ incarnate in the world; the second is a series of human initiatives. The first, which is the church in its truest sense, is that which is not and cannot be built or improved by humans, because it has already been fully established by God in the crucified and risen body of Christ, and it is already present in those who are in union with him through the Holy Spirit. Buildings, budgets, staffs, memberships, denominations—these may be rightful manifestations of the church, but they are not the church itself. For the Christian, they must be considered no more than the human activities of those who are obediently inhabiting the reality of Christ's church. The church is not an institution but an activity—and only secondarily a human one. It is an activity of God done in the lives of his people through Christ and the Spirit.

The lesson here to be observed is that the church, in its fundamental reality, is not something which we in any ultimate sense control.[3] We as humans do not build it or advance it. Nor is there anything which can be done in this world to damage it. It is as firm as God's own throne and unchanging as the one who sits on it. It is not something to be built or advanced or grown or defended, but is an established reality, given by sheer grace. It is something simply to be inhabited and incarnated through daily Christian obedience and love. The question which hangs over the church is not whether we will build it, but whether we will participate in it—indeed, whether it will build us. Every individual believer must decide each day whether he or she will actively live out the reality of Jesus Christ of which they are already a part by his grace.

Ephesians 4 celebrates the church as a gift of God. It is a unity created by that unity which is in God himself, and it flourishes through the various gifts which God bestows upon it through the agency of his redeemed people. Here we see the striking duality of the nature of the church: on the one hand, it has been created and established by God's sovereign grace alone. On the other hand, it calls for human responsibility. That is how God's covenant relationship with his people has always been, with a tension between God's unilateral, unshakable promise, and the human responsibility to live faithfully in light of that promise.

All of this is of critical importance when reflecting on what we have called the problem of the church. It is true that the church which is visible to our eyes is filled with sins and failures. As a human enterprise, what else can we expect? But the problem here is that we have looked to the wrong church—or perhaps we should say, looked at the church wrongly. There really is a church which is accomplishing all that God desires of it, but it is not to be identified with all that is done by humans in the name of the church.

---

3. Here we see the perilous ease through which the church, God's instrument of praise, can become a temple of idols of our own making. When we confuse the church which Christ has built with our own initiatives, we can end up using God's name to validate our own pet projects. This explains the ferocity of some church conflicts: people are not merely having a difference of opinion, but are waging a holy war over a matter they take to be of divine importance. We make the church, its activities, and its methods all about us, and then imbue these human choices with divine significance. It is easy to slip into this with the best of intentions, but it ends up being essentially idolatrous.

Wherever there are human beings inhabiting the righteousness of Jesus Christ in fellowship with one another—and this does really happen—there is the church of which the Scriptures speak.

Right now, we live in the cognitive dissonance between the reality of God's church and all that is faulty in the life of God's people. This dissonance is in fact an essential mark of the experience of God's people, who live in the tension between the "already" and the "not yet." We are learning to become that which we already are; to live properly as inhabitants of that land of which we are already citizens. We are new creation people who still live bodily lives within the old creation, with all the struggles and temptations that accompany it. But the great promise of God is that one day this dissonance will be resolved into harmony. The two churches of which we have spoken—the church of divine activity and the church of human activity—will one day merge into a single reality. That is the day when "the sons of God will be revealed" and all creation will cease its groaning and take up shouts of joyful praise (Rom 8). On that day, we will finally be mature, grown up into the full measure of Jesus Christ, and no longer thrown about on the waves of the fallen world. Yet this is a day we do not merely await with passivity. For us who are in Christ, every day is to be lived as though it were that day, as we strive to enact the reality of what God has done through him.

The Answer Is, and Always has Been, Jesus Christ

These realities of the church, between which there is such tension in the here-and-now, are held together by the grace of God which has appeared in Jesus Christ. Here we encounter a very important part of our answer. The answer to human unrighteousness and unfaithfulness has always ultimately been the righteous and faithfulness of God. This is one of the great themes which spans both the Old Testament and the New. The persistent problem of human unrighteousness is addressed by God himself and his decision to be righteous on our behalf. We see this in Isaiah's theme of the *servant*, the messianic agent of God who enacts all that Israel was meant to do but failed to do. Then in the New Testament we see the servant himself in full clarity: Jesus Christ. God enters into our humanity and therein accomplishes for us what we cannot do for ourselves. In this way God redeemed Israel, and this too is how God redeems his church. In fact, that is precisely what the church is: the community of people who inhabit God's gracious redemption. Our purpose is not to point to our own righteousness, but the righteousness of God in which he has included us by his grace.

And yet, this identity God has given us as bearers of his righteousness does not lead us toward passivity, but toward an active embrace of our own sanctification. God is righteous on our behalf, but his purpose in this is to bring about our actual transformation into the image of Jesus Christ. In other words, God's intention for his people is that they will eventually become in character and behavior that which they already are according to his grace.

The problem of the church remains a matter of our own responsible action

In short, the answer to the problem of the church is the righteousness of God which he has given us in Christ. But this is not an answer which can be used to set aside our own responsibility before God to really live out our identity as his holy people. God has justified sinners, but he has not justified the status quo.

What we have called "the problem of the church" must remain, then, a problem of repentance and responsible action, and not merely a problem of theological reflection. Although all of our above reflections are important for understanding the problem and seeing the answer in Christ, none of these considerations must be taken as excuses for us to avoid the task of reforming the church when this called for. Such avoidance is a denial of the lordship of Jesus Christ and of our responsibility before him.

Of course, we must stand by what has already been said: that the church, in its truest sense, is something which has already been created in Christ once-for-all, and is therefore indestructible. In this sense it is not something which we are responsible to build, for God is building it, and the gates of hell will not stand against it. The church is the manifestation of God's redemptive promise in the world; a promise to which our greatest feats cannot add, and from which our gravest failures cannot subtract. And yet it is a promise in which we dwell according to the obedience which is by faith. The church, in its human sense, is our expression of this faith, and the quality of our life together will show what our faith really is. Is our faith in the work of our own hands—in the power of our preaching; in our boards, budgets, and praise bands? Then we have built in vain, and the lives of our churches will show this. Is our faith in the crucified and resurrected Lord?

This too will show in the life of the community. It will be manifest in the gifts of the Holy Spirit, and above all in mutual, self-sacrificial love. It will be demonstrated in the steadfast maturity whereby we keep our eyes fixed on Christ and his gospel, and not the world's fads which crash against the walls of the church like waves against a rock.

Will Christ's church prevail? Yes—nothing else is possible in God's heaven and earth. Will we live together in the world as true members of this church? Maybe—for this God holds us responsible. But our responsibility is not to point angry fingers at our neighbors (although prophetic words of truth and love are needed in their timely places). We must begin by standing before the mirror of God's word, and asking ourselves: "How am I being faithful to Jesus Christ as a member of his church?"

Conclusion

Throughout our study of Ephesians, we have seen how the gospel is scandalous. God's way in the world is a surprise, and sometimes an outrage, to our natural human sensibilities. We have seen how we as God's people are called to be perpetrators of the scandal. But we have also observed that the church on earth has often been scandalous for all the wrong reasons. Our calling is to reclaim the scandal of the cross as we speak the truth of the gospel with love and seek to embody it in our fellowship together. To do this, we must renounce the scandals by which the church of Christ has been used as an instrument of pride, hatred, and oppression.

History gives us many examples on both sides. The early church was a scandal against the kingdoms of the world when it insisted on practicing hospitality and care for the sick and the outcasts in the Roman empire. But the church became scandalous for all the wrong reasons when it shook hands with political power under Constantine. The Reformation was scandalous as a grace-centered revolt against a church government which had become a system of legalistic oppression and a denial of the gospel. But many heirs of the Reformation created a church which was a scandal against this very gospel when they enshrined the teachings of grace into a new law of institutionalized orthodoxy.[4]

---

4. At various times in which Protestant churches became "dead orthodoxies," various neo-reformers stepped up to reclaim a living faith. These include the pietists (such as Spener, Franke, and Zinzendorf), John Wesley, and Soren Kierkegaard—each, of course, in a very different time and context, but related by some common themes and shared

The Scandal of the Church

In more recent memory, we think about the relationship between the church and the civil rights movement. Perhaps nobody has better exemplified the scandal of the cross than Martin Luther King Jr. in his courageous stand against racial injustice in the American south. He insisted that the church could not merely be a social club for savoring religious niceties. If the church is the body of Christ, it must be on the move against injustice. It must take up its cross and follow Jesus on the way of courageous, loving, self-sacrificial action. But from the point of view of the kingdom, the great scandal was—and perhaps remains—the complicity of the church with a culture of pride and injustice which denied the humanity of non-white people. The church had been blown about by the false teachings of the world; namely the heresy of racism. Martin Luther King Jr. spoke the truth in love and called the church to grow up into the body of Christ; a body which cannot be anything but a unity of diverse people.

That is our calling as God's redeemed-and-redeeming people. It may be difficult to know even where to start in carrying out this work, but Paul offers some great practical instruction on this: "Such a life is marked by humility, gentleness, patience, and bearing with one another in love." In our fellowship with one another, are we humble, gentle, and patient? Do we bear with one another? Do we speak the truth in love? Do we use the gifts that God has given us to build others up? These are beautifully simple instructions which, thoughtfully applied, will take us far.

Heavenly Father, we thank you for the church. We thank you that in the midst of the chaotic world, you have knit us together in Christ, and that in this way you are using us to knit together all things. We thank you for your sacrificial victory in which you have included us, and by which you have so richly bestowed us with gifts.

Lord, we pray that your church would be united and built up, and that in this way we will learn to truly live as your people in the world. Forgive us for our many failings, and by your grace, draw us into your righteousness, that we may attain the full measure of Christ our head. Make us a people set apart from the pride and hatred in the world, so that we might reach out to it as bearers of your humility and love.

Lord, we confess that we your church are not our own: we are the body of Christ, by whose blood we have been purchased. It is in his name that we pray, and in the name of the Spirit who is our unity. Amen.

---

influences.

8
Ethics and the Scandal of the Christian Life

Paraphrase: Ephesians 4:17—5:20

NOW THIS IS WHAT I *affirm and insist on in the Lord: you must no longer live as the gentiles do, nor share in the futility of their thinking. They are darkened in their understanding, and are alienated from the life of God because of their ignorance and hard-heartedness. They have become desensitized and have given themselves over to licentiousness, becoming greedy and full of impurity.*

But that is not the Christ-life you have learned. I know that you have been taught the truth which is in Jesus. You were taught to put away your old life—that old identity which was corrupted and confused by its lusts—and to have a new frame of mind; to put on the identity which has been created in the image of God in true righteousness and holiness. This is what I mean:

- *Reject all falsehood, and speak the truth to one another, for we belong to each other.*
- *Do not let your anger lead you to sin, but deal with it quickly, lest you give the devil a foothold.*
- *Turn away from stealing and do honest work instead—and use what you earn to share with the needy.*
- *Keep your tongue from evil talk, and use your words graciously to build each other up, lest you grieve the Holy Spirit who set you apart for redemption.*

- *Reject all bitterness, anger, vicious slander, and plotting, and embrace kindness, gentleness, and forgiveness, for this is how God has treated you in Christ. In other words, imitate God. After all, you are his children. Live in his love, whereby Christ loved us and gave himself for us as a sacrifice.*
- *Stay away from all kinds of sexual sin, and from all kinds of idolatrous lusts and greediness. These are not fitting for God's holy people. You can be sure that those who embrace that way of life are not part of God's kingdom.*
- *Don't waste your words on foolish chatter and coarse jokes. Save your words for giving thanks.*

Don't be fooled by empty words: it is because of these matters that the disobedient must face God's anger. So do not cast your lot with them. Once you lived in that darkness, but now you live in the light of the Lord. Yes, live as children of light, for light produces all that is good and right and true. Find out what pleases the Lord. Don't take part in the futile works of darkness, but show them for what they are. For we do not even want to talk about the things that the wicked do in secret, but light illuminates everything on which it shines. That is why we say: "Sleeper, awake! Rise from the dead, and let Christ shine on you!"

Therefore, live carefully and wisely, making the most of your time in these evil days. Don't be foolish; know God's desires. Don't get drunk on alcohol (that just leads to more foolishness); drink your fill of the Spirit. Sing psalms, hymns, and spiritual songs together; sing and make music from your heart before the Lord, giving thanks to God the Father at all times and for all things, in the name of our Lord Jesus Christ.

Ephesians 1:4 tells us that "God chose us in Christ before the creation of the world to be holy and blameless before him." We can see how this statement functions, once it is understood in context, as a statement of the main idea of Ephesians. God's eternal purpose has always been to have for himself a people who, in and through their very human personhood, reflect his goodness, wisdom, and love in relationship with him and one another. The problem of human sin is such that we have instead used the freedom given to us to engage in a rebellion against God. God's solution, in which he restores humanity to their purpose in creation, is the God-man Jesus Christ. In him, God is righteous, holy, and loving on behalf of an unrighteous people. But this strategy of redemption is two-fold: God not only wants to graciously forgive unrighteous people, but in the end, to actually make these people righteous. In Christ, God treats caterpillars as though they were butterflies, but his end goal is really to make them sprout wings and fly. By drawing us into union with Jesus Christ, God's intent is not only that we will benefit from his righteousness, but that we will, by living within the new reality he has created for us, learn to be like him. To use theological language, justification must never be separated from its goal of sanctification. The cross of Christ means both atonement and discipleship. It is a cross he bore for us, but he also means for us to take it up and carry it. Without putting both of these truths together, we will have an inadequate grasp of the Christian faith.

Unfortunately, we have the tendency to emphasize one side of this at the expense of the other. When we emphasize only justification, we create a church that is content with the status quo, both with respect to the state of our own souls and the condition of the world around us. Here we create a church whose only job is to preach a gospel of cheap grace. Such churches may become licentious, believing that grace means "anything goes." But cheap grace can also take a surprisingly legalistic form. Churches that preach only justification can end up condemning all those who don't spell out their theology of grace and atonement exactly as they do. Salvation by grace alone can be turned into salvation by agreement-with-our-particular-doctrine alone. Here grace becomes ungracious.

But when we emphasize only sanctification, we create a church which demands fresh water from a blocked-up well. The church that merely preaches righteous behavior misses the gospel; therefore they not only miss out on grace, but also even the righteous behavior they seek, which has no source but the transforming work of Christ on our behalf. Legalism undermines love, and therefore it kills both the tree and its fruit. In destroying the gospel, it also, ironically, destroys the kind of good works which God has prepared in advance for us to do.

In Ephesians 4:17—5:20, we see a sketch of justification and sanctification working harmoniously together in the Christian life. This is real sanctification, and not just a legal fiction. There really is a difference in the entire manner and shape of the Christian's life compared to what they were. But it is a difference which stands on the foundation of God's work in Christ rather than our own initiative. Paul doesn't say "Sinners, stop being sinners and give yourself a new identity and way of life." Instead he says, "Because

Ethics and the Scandal of the Christian Life

of Christ, you have been given a new identity and way of life. Therefore, stop sinning. Stop living according to what you used to be, and start living according to what God in his grace has already made you to be." Again, we are reminded of the meaning of Christian sanctification: learning bit-by-bit to become in daily life that which we already are according to God's grace.

This means that while Christianity is not primarily about ethics, it is inescapably ethical in character. The heart and center of the Christian faith is not a code of ethical behavior, but rather an act of God through Jesus Christ, to which we respond in faith. It is not a legalistic religion, but a lived relation. This is the fine line on which we stand: that the Christian faith is not founded or centered on our lived behavior, yet it cannot be expressed or fulfilled any other way. To use biblical language, we are saved by faith and not by works, but faith without works is dead. Or, as the reformers said, we are saved by faith alone, but saving faith is never alone. Faith is not faith if it does not end up penetrating all aspects of our human existence, including that of our daily life. Ephesians 4:17—5:20 invites us to explore the distinct meaning of Christian ethics: the living of our faith in daily life.

The Uniqueness of Christian Ethics: Discipleship, Allegiance, and Love

A clear instance of modern short-sightedness is the philosophical belief that we should (and even can) separate the questions of ethics from those of ultimate reality (what philosophers call metaphysics or ontology). Ethics, as a branch of philosophy, is basically just an attempt to answer the questions "What is good?" and "How do we embrace the good in our societies and personal lives?" On the face of it, these seem like much more practical and answerable questions than ones such as "What is the nature of ultimate reality" or "Is there a God?" Unfortunately, it is sometimes forgotten that the answer to the question "What is good?" depends very much on our answers to those more metaphysical questions.

Now, it is true that we can talk about goodness and morality on a purely experiential level, apart from metaphysical claims, because humans are inherently morally-aware creatures. That is why people of all beliefs (whether of a religious or irreligious nature) can agree that murder, for example, is morally wrong. But apart from the questions of ultimate reality, we never know exactly what we are talking about when we use words like "morally" and "wrong." Is our abhorrence of murder just something practical, a matter of instinct or tastefulness? Or, is it grounded in an eternal reality beyond us? Is it rooted in the authority and character of God? It is possible that people who answer those questions very differently might end up behaving quite the same, but the meaning behind their behavior will be very different. For example, atheists are usually, by my observation, very moral people. The problem is that, according to their own worldview, they do not have good reason to be. This begs the question: how long can we maintain a moral life or a moral society on the basis of the presupposition that reality itself is ultimately amoral? How long, after convincing ourselves that we have no souls, can we keep living as though we do? It matters tremendously how we think. It is important for its own sake, but also for the implications regarding how we live.

Ephesians 4 tells us that there is something radically different about how a Christian thinks. Paul tells his audience that they previously were darkened in their understanding, being ignorant and hard-hearted. (That is not a flattering description! It is noteworthy that Paul is telling his audience how to think of their own former identities, not how to talk to their unbelieving neighbors.) Here we are reminded of Paul's famous instruction in Romans 12: "Do not be conformed to the pattern of this world, but be transformed by the renewal of your mind." The transformation involved in sanctification involves a new way of thinking; a new perspective or outlook on life. This is a truth confirmed by much experience of those who have been trapped in destructive or self-defeating behaviors: that as long as we keep thinking the same, we will act the same, and we will not start acting differently until we learn to think differently.

Specifically, Paul reminds his audience that they have "learned Christ." They are meant to look at life through a set of Jesus-shaped glasses. Perhaps better, we could say that they are to look at the world through new eyes— eyes which have beheld Christ and are therefore Christlike. That is, they are to see things from the vantage point of their new, true identity which has been created in Jesus Christ. A Christian is someone who, by being restored as an image-bearer of God after the pattern of Christ, has a new vantage point by which to understand himself or herself, and in this way to have a new outlook on life. This involves the questions of ethics: judgements about what is good and how to live out that goodness in the context of our relational worlds.

This passage lists many particular instructions for Christian living, and most of them appear to be rather conventional. Neither Jesus nor Paul had any intention of introducing a novel system of right and wrong. We should be careful to remember that neither of them saw moral teaching as the center of their ministry. Jesus's mission was to come as the king who establishes his kingdom by works of love, self-sacrifice, and resurrection. Paul's mission was to testify about the reality of this kingdom to the gentiles and invite them to become a part of it, thereby building God's church. Teachings about how humans are to live come after, and not before, the declarations of what God has done. The New Testament's teaching about how to live a virtuous life does not introduce any completely new moral ideas (although every human culture or generation finds at least some of them controversial). The surprise of Christian ethics lies not so much in its content, but in its uniquely Christ-initiated basis and character. In other words, Paul's ethical instructions are striking not so much because of the kind of behaviors they call for, but because they are so much more than instructions on living a good life; they are in fact a rather ordinary expression of a whole new way of being human in the world before God. We could say that these instructions are the conventional tip of a revolutionary iceberg. We will see this as we examine three ideas which give Christian ethics its distinct foundation and character: discipleship, allegiance, and love.[1]

Discipleship

"But that is not the Christ-life you have learned," Paul says. Or to render it more literally: "that is not how you learned Christ." Paul goes on to talk about learning the true way of life and attitude which comes from Jesus and is modeled after him. In other words, Paul is talking about discipleship. Discipleship means a process, or a way of life, in which a person learns from a teacher. But our words *learn* and *teacher* here lose something in their modern connotations. This is not merely about the communication of information, but about the transformation of character. Discipleship involves sitting at the feet of a master and learning from him or her, so that the student not only knows what the master knows, but grows to become a similar kind of person, even as the student keeps his or her individuality.

We find a somewhat similar idea in Aristotle's *Ethics*, in which he emphasizes the development of a set of moderate, well-rounded virtues. He indicates that a virtuous life is built up through personal discipline.[2] This

---

1. This is not meant to be an exhaustive list, just a good start.
2. Aristotle, *Ethics*, 334.

process has as its goal the actualization of *happiness*, which for Aristotle had the distinct meaning of becoming a complete, whole, well-ordered person. He often defined happiness as "an activity of the soul in conformity with complete virtue." In this way, he brought together virtuous actions and a blessed state of being, in which a person has attained a state of completion or actualization and acts this out in daily life. Here a person has become a student of reason and the laws of nature, so as to become in their activity that which they already are by virtue of being human.

All of this has some interesting similarities to the Christian idea of sanctification and discipleship, but with at least one very important difference. The Christian is not (necessarily) a student of our own nature or a rational natural law which points us toward a complete, virtuous existence, but is (necessarily) a student of a particular person: Jesus Christ.[3] Of course, Aristotle could well agree with the need for a human teacher to assist us on this quest of personal discipline. Here we think of Socrates and his disciples. But Jesus, unlike such teachers, was unique in that he was not only the teacher but also the lesson. Other teachers, mentors, and masters teach their students about something else; Jesus called people to come and learn *him*. Jesus was not merely a prophet who disclosed truths from God; he himself was the revelation and the truth of God which was taught. That is why Paul can make the striking statement that the Ephesians have "learned Christ."

This is the unique ethical implication of Christian discipleship: that God's people are not merely meant to be followers of a moral code, but followers of a person; namely, Jesus Christ. In doing so, God's people see themselves not just as imitators of a good example for human life (though this is surely an important part of it), but as humans formed after a kind of life initiated by God himself, their creator. Again, this may not make the content of Christian ethics markedly different in all cases, but it gives them a very unique basis. We understand right and wrong not only as norms for how the world works best, or as a natural law, but as something deriving from the personal character and desires of the creator, made visible and manifest in Jesus Christ, for us to follow. Here we see that the significance of discipleship to Christ is twofold, because Christians confess that Jesus is both fully divine and fully human. In him, God has revealed both perfect

---

3. Although of course the Christian, by implication, should be both. Because we are disciples of the living God made flesh, we are students of all his creational intentions for the world and our lives.

divinity and perfect humanity. Christ is both the image of the invisible God, and the ideal human image-bearer. Discipleship to Christ means learning how to live as God's human image-bearers, and therefore to resemble and participate in the very goodness of God, in our own finite measure.

Allegiance

To be a disciple of Jesus Christ is also to be a member of that solidarity which figured so strongly in his teaching: the kingdom of God. This is another way in which the distinctively personal character of Christian ethics plays out: it is not only about personal discipleship to Christ as our teacher, but also personal allegiance to him as our king. In this sense, Christian ethics is not merely a matter of the behaviors we adopt, but also a matter of which side we are on in a clash between kingdoms. This is one of the reasons why simply seeking to be a good person, apart from Christ, misses the point according to a Christian view of salvation. It is possible to deliver the service of good behavior for the sake of the wrong kingdom. This is a fact which should be taken to heart, not only by unbelievers, but also by those who consider themselves Christians. Yes, they have "done the right things." They have put on their best Christian behavior. They have said the prayer. But do they really belong to Jesus Christ? Are they on his side of the battle lines?

This is a sobering question which calls to mind one of the more alarming statements in Scripture, spoken by Jesus himself: "Many will say to me on that day, 'Lord, Lord, did we not prophesy in your name and in your name drive out demons, and in your name perform many miracles?' Then I will tell them plainly, 'I never knew you. Away from me, you evildoers!'" (Matt 7:22–24). After all, it is not right behavior which puts us on the right side of God, but living faith. We are reminded of what Paul has already said: "It is by grace you are saved, through faith. None of this was your own doing, but is God's gift." It is only by God's grace that we come over to the right side of the battle, and that grace is only received through faith.

At this point it may be tempting to completely give up on the task of articulating a Christian ethic. It can seem like the gospel actually tears down the foundation for ethical behavior. It may in fact tear down certain foundations, such as those based on systems of merit and reward. But here we need the reminder that God's grace-through-faith has as its goal and outworking the "good works prepared in advance for us to do." Because this is the case, we can in fact infer a connection between Christian identity and Christian behavior, but the connection is the reverse of what is sometimes supposed. Christian behavior is not the cause of salvation; rather salvation is the cause of Christian behavior. Therefore, the way we live our lives can function as evidence for the real quality of our faith and allegiance to Jesus Christ. We don't get into the kingdom by exhibiting the right behaviors, but if anyone really lives a kingdom life, we can interpret that as evidence of a faith-relation to God. On the other hand, the claim of Christian faith may be suspect for the person who never really lives as though Jesus is their teacher and lord.

This helps us understand the language in this chapter which perhaps smells of "works salvation" to many protestants: "You can be sure that those who embrace that way of life are not part of God's kingdom." "It is because of these matters that the disobedient must face God's anger." The ethics of the Christian life are serious business, not because they are prerequisites for God's love, but because they are its inevitable result. A life which is marked by ongoing, persistent rebellion against God is one which has not, according to the evidence, been touched by the transforming love of God. This love, which birthed whole worlds, has conceived a new creature in those formed after the pattern of Jesus Christ. The Christian has a new identity and belongs to a new circle of solidarity. This is why we must no longer cast our lot with the kingdoms of darkness from whence we were drawn.

It is worth thinking through the ethical implications of all this. That is precisely what Paul does in listing various elements of Christian behavior. As we have said, the morality outlined here may not be unique (although it may run against the grain of our own culture on more than one point), but its basis certainly is. For comparison, we can think of some of the chief schools of ethical thought which have been emphasized throughout the history of philosophy. These include virtue ethics, such as Aristotle emphasized (with a focus on the development of virtuous character in alignment with reason), the ethics of conformity to absolute rules for their own sake (as Kant emphasized), or the more practical-minded school of utilitarianism, urging us to calculate what will result in the greatest good for the greatest number.[4] Christians can and should learn something from each of these schools of thought. We should be interested in character development, devoted to God's moral law, and concerned for the practical good of

---

4. For a helpful summary of traditional models of ethics from a Christian point of view, see Reuschling, *Reviving Evangelical Ethics*.

the world around us. But for Christians there is a key difference: all of this is intensely personal. Ethics are not, at bottom, about actualizing impersonal goods, following impersonal rules, or pursuing impersonal goals for worldly improvement. It's all about personal allegiance to the King of Kings. We seek to do the right thing not according to the logic of an impersonal code, but rather that of personal loyalty and devotion. We desire not to betray our best friend not merely because doing so goes against a moral law (although that is the case), but also because of our personal love and devotion to our friend. For the Christian, all matters of right and wrong take on that kind of personal hue. We want to resist falsehood, theft, treachery, and lust not only because they are bad for us, not only because they are bad for the world, and not only because they go against the moral law known by our conscience, but in addition, because they are a betrayal of the Lord we love.

The context of Christian ethics is the clash between kingdoms, and we have been redeemed by King Jesus to fight alongside him. (This means we need to wear the armor of God, but we will get to that later.) Right now, we want to consider what this means for Christian life in this world. Throughout the book of Ephesians, we have repeatedly caught glimpses of the fact that in this world there is a battle which rages between the forces of the true king and those of the realms, authorities, powers, and dominions. We need to learn to see the world in this light. Of course, people are not the enemy—we do not fight against flesh and blood. But all humans are naturally caught up in this struggle both as victims of evil and as coconspirators with it. We therefore desire to see people as God sees them: as lost but loved image-bearers and objects of God's redeeming mission.

Seeing the world through this lens should make us more aware of the structures of pride, injustice, and oppression in the world, and to understand the prophetic role of Christian ethics in this context. For us, ethics are not merely a matter of personal behavior. The church is called to incarnate the spirit of the words from Isaiah which Jesus quoted to summarize his mission to redeem Israel from exile:

> *The Spirit of the Lord is on me,*
> *because he has anointed me to proclaim good news to the poor.*
> *He has sent me to proclaim freedom for the prisoners*
> *and recovery of sight for the blind,*
> *to set the oppressed free,*
> *to proclaim the year of the Lord's favor.* (Luke 4:17–19)

In other words, Christians belong to another kingdom, but this does not make us neutral in regard to the suffering and injustice on earth. Our ethics are lived out not only with respect for moral principles, but also personal allegiance to the Lord of all righteousness—and therefore allegiance to the people he loves.

In one respect, therefore, Christian ethics bears an uncanny resemblance to another ethical system: Marxism. This is an alarming thing to say, since the political legacy of Marxism over the last century has been anything but ethical. But Marxism, like Christianity, understands ethics in the context of allegiances in a power struggle between solidarities (kingdoms, to use Christian language.) Namely, Marxism sees life as a struggle between an oppressive owner class and an oppressed worker class. Marxism is also an essentially eschatological belief system, as is Christianity: they both look forward to an age of consummation in which all wrongs will be righted.[5]

However, there are very important differences between Christianity and Marxism; differences which illustrate essential elements of Christian ethics. Marxism is fundamentally humanistic, and its eschatology depends on the working-class taking matters into their own hands and inaugurating the hypothetical blessed age through the power of revolution. Christians also look forward to a revolution in which love, goodness, and peace will triumph over hatred, evil, and oppression. But this revolution is God-initiated. It has already begun through Jesus Christ, and it will be consummated by his power. Although we are called to actively live it out through daily works of love, it is not up to us to overthrow the kingdoms of the world. We await the kingdom of the one who has already conquered through the cross.

Secondly, while Marxism correctly sees life on earth as a power struggle between good and evil, it draws the battle lines too simplistically. According to Marxism, the oppressed are good and the oppressors are evil. Both of those judgements are correct as far as they go, but the full reality is far more complex. All humans, oppressed and oppressor alike, are God's good creation—that is why oppression is evil. Yet all people, oppressed and oppressor together, are naturally participants in an evil rebellion against

---

5. This comparison between Christianity and Marxism is relevant because some liberation theologies, which have sought to engage in theology deliberately on the foundation of the experience of oppressed peoples, are deeply influenced by Marxism; namely by its tendency to see reality strictly through the binary grid of victims and oppressors. Influential examples include Gutierrez, *Theology of Liberation,* and Cone, *Black Theology and Black Power.*

God. This is why, to be blunt, Marxism doesn't work. It is a revolt against tyranny which only results in a new set of oppressors. History seems to have repeated itself again and again on this point. This is a fact about which Christians should be sorrowful, but not surprised. Here we remember two great scandals of the Christian faith: the belief that anyone, down to the most innocent child, is capable of being a wicked tyrant if given the opportunity, but that everyone—including the wickedest tyrants—are beloved creatures of God whom he wants to redeem. Marxism, like most worldly philosophies, has no room for the scandal of the doctrine of sin, nor for the scandal of grace. But for those who grasp them, these twin outrages converge into a single river called mercy.

Of course, Christian theology presents us with a dangerous temptation at this point: to relativize and trivialize all the oppressions of the world. It is tempting for us (especially those of us who enjoy a privileged position) to say "everyone's a sinner, not just the tyrants, so let them be. God loves them too." But God's love, tolerant as it may be during this present season of his patience, never winks at evil. His love is too pure to tolerate any wickedness in its object. In eternity, our wickedness will either be separated from us and destroyed (the device of this separation being Christ's sacrifice on the cross), or we will keep our wickedness and be destroyed ourselves. In the long run, those are the only alternatives. This matter of eternal justice demands our present and urgent attention, firstly with respect to our own sanctification, and secondly with respect to calling out and fighting against the injustices of our world. So we agree with Paul: "Don't take part in the futile works of darkness, but show them for what they are. For we do not even want to talk about the things that the wicked do in secret, but light illuminates everything on which it shines. That is why we say: "Sleeper, awake! Rise from the dead, and let Christ shine on you!"

Love

Like Marxism, then, Christian ethics must take sides. We must stand with God against the powers of evil which work their way in the world, and that includes all evils of oppression and injustice. We take sides with the poor, the downtrodden, the sick, the alien, and the marginalized. We fight with them, and for them.

But the weapons by which we fight, and the goals to which we aspire, are very different than those wielded by the world (and certainly by

Marxism). Our tool is not the violent revolution led by those who demand their rights, but the revolution of love, led by the one who laid all his rights down and went to the cross for his enemies. Our goal is not to give oppressors a taste of their own medicine while the oppressed have their fun for a change. The goal is to bring all humans, the sinners and the sinned-against, to the foot of the cross, where we will understand that we all belong to a single class: lost but loved creatures of God. Only the cross can at once tear down the pride of the powerful and lift up the despair of the desolate. Only then will we be, once again, merely but magnificently human.

We are reminded here of the words of one of the greatest communicators and enactors of Christian ethics during the past century: Martin Luther King Jr. He famously said, "Darkness cannot drive out darkness, only light can do that. Hatred cannot drive out hatred, only love can do that." Or as Paul put it in Romans 12, where he explains at length the meaning of sincere love, "Do not be overcome by evil, but overcome evil with good."

As it turns out, love is the real essence of Christian ethics. This point emerges at the heart of Paul's list of instructions for Christian behavior: "Embrace kindness, gentleness, and forgiveness, for this is how God has treated you in Christ. In other words, imitate God. After all, you are his children. Live in his love, whereby Christ loved us and gave himself for us as a sacrifice." Christians are those who have experienced the extravagant love of God in Christ and who therefore turn to face the world with this same attitude. We are also reminded of what Jesus affirmed as the two greatest commandments which summarize the whole of the law and the prophets: to love God completely and to love our neighbors as ourselves (Matt 22:36-40). While Christianity doesn't introduce a novel system of ethics, it is still revolutionary in calling us to live a life of radical love, even to the counterintuitive extent of loving our enemies.[6]

The significance of this is both potent and far-reaching for our understanding of Christian ethics. At bottom, the ethics of the Christian faith are not about following an impersonal command. They are not merely about

---

6. Of course, we should also note the significance of Jesus's Sermon on the Mount in Matthew 5-7 as central and distinctive to Christian ethics. These are not given attention here, where focus is more specifically on Paul's argument in Ephesians. But a few quick observations should be made about the Sermon on the Mount which align with the claims of this chapter. First, Jesus's sermon focuses on the kingdom of God, which is the unique realm in the context of which we understand Christian behavior. Second, Jesus's sermon gives self-sacrificial love (even for our enemies) pride of place. Third, the Sermon on the Mount reinforces our conviction that Jesus is both our teacher (from whom we learn as disciples) and our Lord (who uniquely enacted the truths he proclaimed).

doing the most good in a general sense to make the world a better place. They aren't even fundamentally about character development as we learn to be more virtuous people. Christian ethics do include all of these, but their living heart is the reenactment of the love which has been given to us by our creator and redeemer, in the context of his inbreaking kingdom.

Of course, merely invoking the word *love* doesn't solve all our ethical dilemmas and complex moral issues. In the face of the world's conflicts and sufferings, it will not do to simply say, "Let's just love each other." Perhaps an oversimplified, sentimentalized view of love is actually a great moral blindness of our age. But this is not a case of too much love. Rather, we have seen too little of the genuine article to be able to properly recognize it and put it in action. Real love knows how to be tender and tough-as-nails at the same time.

Perhaps love can be defined more or less this way: an active commitment to the ultimate good of another person. It is a concern for others which is not only felt but enacted. And, it is not enacted only when felt, but consistently, according to a steadfast commitment. It is also rooted in the reality of *goodness*: there is no love apart from the moral framework in which we can meaningfully understand and act for another person's true good. Authentic love, as a thoroughgoing commitment to the real good of others, therefore calls us deeper into the hard ethical questions regarding the nature of goodness. To love cannot really mean always to be smiling and nodding, offering our easy approval to all ideas and choices we encounter. Such assumptions about the nature of love, prevalent as they may be in our contemporary discourse, do nothing but impoverish our understanding and practice of it.

But although love may never be a substitute for hard and clear ethical thinking, love must never be absent from it. That is a point just as frequently forgotten as the fact of love's moral hardness. Our ethical thinking—particularly our *Christian* ethical thinking—cannot in any event be reduced to an impersonal application of moral rules. If our ethic is rooted in love, we will never overlook the basic but often neglected task of simply caring about people. If sloppy assumptions about love are a problem in our modern discourse, the failure to simply care about other people—and treat them like real persons—is another. Here I do not mean a theoretical caring for people in the abstract, which is often used as an excuse to abuse and disrespect the people who are actually standing in front of us. Consider, for example, all the attention which Paul places in this passage on judicious and loving use of language. For the Christian, winning an argument must never be a priority over communicating respect and compassion to others at all times. Perhaps in many cases the argument which is won by our cleverness and celebrated by our pride is deemed by God a tragic loss.[7] It is possible that simple kindness to others in our words and actions is more valuable in his sight than anything we might accomplish in the public cultural discourse. That is not an excuse to neglect the latter (which is also an important dimension of love for our neighbors), but simply a reminder to keep things first things first. Otherwise we invoke upon ourselves the warnings Jesus made about gaining the world but losing our souls. Perhaps we overestimate God's interest in cultural monuments. What he wants are a few good people—people who walk with him in daily faith and who love their neighbors in word and deed.

Once again, our understanding of love is never adequate without contemplating the cross. This is the supreme enactment of the love whereby we have been loved. It is the self-sacrificial act of God which has redeemed us and established the reality in which we live—and the perspective by which we see the world. This calls us to embrace that scandalous paradox by which we set ourselves apart from the world—that great kingdom of "power-against"—precisely by loving the world radically, taking on the Christ-like, self-emptying attitude of "power-for." The triumph of Christian ethics, then, is not a new season of political victory or cultural progress, but something somehow far greater: the giving of a cup of cold water to a person God loves. We find ourselves called to be an odd people (as Dorothy Sayers said, "The truth will make you odd.") Our particular way of life cannot comfortably fit into the ways of the world. Sometimes we find ourselves celebrating things the world rejects and rejecting things the world celebrates. But if Christians are to be known in the world—known, that is, with any accuracy regarding our true identity in Christ—we will be known for our love.

The Holy Spirit

There is a final unique element to a Christian view of ethics, and that has to do with the conviction expressed throughout the New Testament that God's people are not merely living in reflection of God hovering distantly above them, but rather that God is dwelling with them—even *in* them. The

---

7. C. S. Lewis makes this point in his poem "Apologist's Evening Prayer," 129.

Ethics and the Scandal of the Christian Life

Christian life and ethic is a practice of the presence of God; a daily enactment of our union with him. We are in God and God is in us. This is the doctrine of the Holy Spirit.

This is perhaps one of the most neglected doctrines throughout the whole history of the church. The last century has seen a revival of joyful attention to the power and presence of the Holy Spirit in the Pentecostal movement. But for many other branches of God's church, the Holy Spirit remains a shadowy figure. We know, through all our ancient and modern church confessions, that the Spirit is a person of the Trinity and is therefore just as much God as the Father and the Son. But we don't know quite what to do with him. We have a clear place for the other members of the Godhead. The Father governs the universe in mighty providence. The Son saves us, intercedes for us, and rules the kingdom of which we are members. But what does the Spirit do? Perhaps he gives us encouragements or moral nudges from time to time, but not much else.

But how wrong we are about this. The question is not in what part of God's rule and the Christian life the Spirit is involved, but whether there is any part in which he isn't. The Holy Spirit is the one in whom we share union with the crucified and resurrected Christ, and therefore the one in whom we enjoy blessed sonship-and-daughtership to the God of all glory. (Notice here that Father, Son, and Holy Spirit all play a crucial role in our salvation. We could say that atonement was a trinitarian conspiracy of grace). As the source and power of our union with God, the presence and activity of the Spirit underlies every aspect of the Christian life. We should note that Paul refers to the Holy Spirit numerous times throughout Ephesians (at least 13). For Paul, our union with God and one another, the promise of membership in the age to come, our share in the knowledge and power of God, are all through the Holy Spirit.

It is no surprise, then, that Paul concludes this section devoted to sanctification and the norms of the Christian life with a stirring call to rejoice in the Spirit. He uses striking language that suggests getting drunk on the Spirit rather than on alcoholic beverage. The presence of the Spirit in our lives, however, is not a befuddling intoxication, but on the contrary gives us uniquely sharpened moral vision and ethical reflexes. In fact, we need the Holy Spirit to understand and embody the wisdom of God in the midst of these "evil days."

We are reminded also of Paul's instruction in Galatians: "Walk by the Spirit, and you will not gratify the cravings of the sinful nature" (Gal 5:16).

In this context, life in the Spirit is juxtaposed not only with life in the flesh, or the sinful nature, but life in the law. Paul argues that God's ultimate solution to the problem of bondage to the norms of a lost and rebellious world is not the external power and covenantal identity associated with Israel's law, but rather the inward power and Christ-defined identity which God's people of faith possess through the Holy Spirit.

This has powerful implications for the ethical vision of God's people. As stressed above, the uniqueness of Christian ethics lies less in its particular content than in its orientation toward discipleship to Christ, its basis in allegiance to his kingdom, and its focus on cruciform love. These dimensions of the Christian life are realized, however, only by the power of the Spirit; God in us. Here we see that the good life, from the standpoint of God's holy people in Christ, is not ultimately a matter of conformity to a list of moral rules or a humanistic enterprise for earthly flourishing, but membership in God's kingdom, discipleship to Jesus Christ, and participation in a story of redeeming love, all in union with God and his people by the power of his Holy Spirit.

Conclusion

Paul's admonitions to the Ephesians are, in one sense, very simple. He calls the people of God to live a life together of clear-headed honesty, responsible and judicious use of our words, chaste use of our bodies, humble diligence, and everyday patience and kindness to one another from a sincere heart. Not the building of an empire; not sociopolitical supremacy; not crushing arguments to forever silence all opposition and all doubt. Just simple, sacrificial love, in humble, steadfast devotion to the one who so perfectly enacted it on our behalf.

Yet in all its simplicity, this is how God's great and scandalous plan goes forward. Ordinary people—fallen people, lost people, loved people—stepping into the circle of light which God has shined on the world through Christ, and learning to live and love like him by the power of the Holy Spirit. This is how God loves the world. This is how we become human. This is how the powers of darkness are confronted. This is how the kingdom conquers. This is how God's eternal purpose for the universe unfolds.

Father, we give you praise for creating us: not merely for forming our bodies and placing us in this world, but for creating us anew in Jesus Christ by the power of the Holy Spirit. We praise you for drawing us into his identity; for giving us not only a new life, but giving us life itself. Our prayer, O Lord, is that you, having given us this life, will now teach us how to live. Make us every day more like Jesus. We praise you for giving him to us as our savior. Help us now to live before him as our daily teacher and our eternal Lord. Teach us what it means to belong to your kingdom even as we exist within this world. Above all, Lord, teach us to love. Teach us to love you above all, and to love others the way you have loved us. In this way, Father, make us, your church, the instrument of your love, your peace, and your reign over all. May your eternal purposes, in which you have so graciously involved us, go forward, for the praise of your glory and the honor of your name. We pray in the name of Jesus Christ and the Holy Spirit, in whom we forever rejoice. Amen!

9

Christian Relationships and the Scandal of Submission

Paraphrase: Ephesians 5:21—6:9

SUBMIT TO ONE ANOTHER *out of reverence for Christ.*

Wives, submit to your husbands, as to the Lord. For the husband is the head of his wife like Christ is the head of his church. The church is Christ's body, and he is her savior. In the way that the church submits to Christ, so let wives submit to their husbands. Husbands, love your wives, just as Christ loved his church and sacrificially laid himself down for her. He did this to sanctify her by cleansing her with water through the word, so that she could be presented to him in splendor; spotless and holy, without any flaw or blemish. This is how husbands should love their wives: as their own bodies. The man who loves his wife loves himself. No one hates their own body, but cares and provides for it. That is what Christ did for his body, the church, to which we belong as members. Remember what was written: "For this reason a man will leave his father and mother and be united to his wife, and the two will become one flesh." This is a profound mystery, which concerns not only husbands and wives, but also Christ and his body, the church. But the application is this: husbands should love their wives as they love themselves, and wives should respect their husbands.

Children, submit to your parents as to the Lord, for this is right. "Honor your father and mother." This commandment is the first of the ten to come with a promise attached: "So that it may be well with you and you may live long on the earth." Parents, do not provoke your children to anger, but bring

Christian Relationships and the Scandal of Submission

them up in the loving discipline and instruction which you yourselves have received from the Lord.

Slaves, submit to your earthly masters with proper reverence, with a heart of undivided obedience to Christ. Do not just work for the eyes of your earthly master, but for the eyes of Christ, who is your true master. Give heartfelt service, as to the Lord and not to human beings, because everyone, whether slave or free, receives their reward from God. Masters, do likewise for your slaves. Do not threaten them, for you know that there is but one master in heaven, and he shows no partiality between you.

Throughout our study of Ephesians, we have already seen how significantly human persons figure into God's plan for the universe, in which he means to put his goodness, wisdom, and love on display. As we have seen, God's purpose is not merely to pull people into this plan as individuals, but to create a new social solidarity of people who share a common union with Christ—such a union that they can be described as his body. Because humans are social creatures, our redemption cannot be anything less than a renewed community. In fact, this renewal of human fellowship is a central aspect of God's whole endeavor. Humans are made in the image of the trinitarian God, and are designed to inhabit a network of loving relationships. To exist in such a fellowship is an essential aspect of what it means to be human. The destruction of human relations has been a chief outcome of our fall into sin, and the restoration of these relations is one of the chief aspects of our redemption. Once again, God will have (and, we believe, already has) a community of people whose loving fellowship is a participation in that which has existed eternally in the Trinity.

Christian existence is therefore necessarily relational in character. But Paul does not merely have what we would call "church relations" in mind. For persons who have received the love of God, every relationship is seen in its light. We could extend this even to so slight a relationship as the meeting of a stranger's eyes when passing in the street. For us, this person is not a nameless object, but a beloved bearer of the divine image, whom Christ died to save and restore as a vessel of eternal glory. It could be worthwhile to develop the spiritual discipline of praying a quick prayer for every person we come across—perhaps just looking their way and saying in our heart, "Lord, may this person know your truth and your love today."

But the relations of particular interest to Paul in this passage are those which occupy so much of our everyday lives: family and household relations. These include the relationship of husband and wife, parent and child, and (more awkwardly for today's context) slave and master. We remember that slaves were commonly members of households in the context of Paul's audience. It is astonishing to us that Paul can be so nonchalant about what seems an inherently abusive, unjust, and oppressive social practice as slavery. Perhaps what is even more surprising is the notion that even a relation such as this can be reconstituted on the basis of the love of Jesus Christ.[1]

Mutual Submission and the Reenactment of Divine Relationships

This is in fact the basis of all the relationships which Paul discusses. All of his instructions for spouses, parents/children, and slaves/masters have their root in a deceptively simple command: "Submit to one another out of reverence for Christ."

Paul begins with the instruction that wives should submit to their husbands—an idea which would have seemed normal at the time but sounds terribly regressive to modern Western people. However, even if it was normal enough thousands of years ago for wives to have a subservient relationship to their husbands, Paul gives a basis for this relationship which is nothing short of countercultural, for then as much as now. Notice that Paul says nothing about a natural hierarchy. He does not say "Wives, submit to your husband, because he is your social superior according to the laws of nature."[2] He says, "Wives, submit to your husbands, as to the Lord." He goes on to make an extended analogy between the husband-wife relation and the Christ-church relation. In doing so, he provides an explicitly theological rationale for the wife's submission, grounded not in the natural social order but in the salvation given by Jesus Christ. Paul is not telling women to

---

1. The danger of this statement is its power in providing an excuse. We can easily imagine a nineteenth-century American slaveowner saying that slavery is fine with God so long as the masters treat their slaves in a loving way. But what really is a loving way to treat a person over whom you have absolute mastery, other than to set them free? That is the eventual logical outcome of Paul's argument. Without calling for the abolition of slavery, Paul sets forth a new norm for relationships which will inevitably lead there. In the long run, slavery and an ethic of humble love cannot coexist. One will eventually destroy the other.

2. See Foster, *Celebration of Discipline*, 117–18.

preserve the cultural status quo, but to take part in a symbolic performance of the relationship between humanity and God.

The trouble here is that such a relationship between husbands and wives appears to be one-sided in terms of power and authority. Not only does that endorse the patriarchal status quo which has been typical even down to the present time; it also seems to create a haven for abuse, whether physical or emotional.

But Paul's analogy won't allow this. Notice that he doesn't say "Wives, submit to your husbands, and husbands, make sure that your wives toe the line." Instead, he calls husbands and wives to take an equal part in this rehearsal of Christ's love. Husbands are not called to enforce a social hierarchy, but to love their wives as Christ loves the church. And how, exactly, has Christ loved the church? Sacrificially, or, we could even say, submissively.

We are helped here by Philippians 2:2–8, in which believers are urged to imitate the humility and servitude of Christ:

> *Do nothing out of selfish ambition or vain conceit. Rather, in humility value others above yourselves, not looking to your own interests, but each of you to the interests of the others. In your relationships with one another, have the same mindset as Christ Jesus:*
> *Who, being in very nature God,*
> *did not consider equality with God something to be used for his own advantage;*
> *rather, he made himself nothing by taking the very nature of a servant,*
> *being made in human likeness.*
> *And being found in appearance as a man,*
> *He humbled himself by becoming obedient to death—*
> *Even to death on a cross!*

Here in Philippians, Paul says nothing about specific relationships, such as between husbands and wives, but this is the relational ethic which seems to lie behind his more specific instructions in Ephesians and elsewhere. Christians are called to inhabit the relational world created by Jesus Christ in his ministry of self-sacrificial love and servanthood. It is a way of seeing ourselves and others which should come to define all our relationships, and we see Paul unpack this in Ephesians 5:21—6:9. Husbands, wives, parents, children, slaves, and masters are all called to enact these relational roles, not according the natural pattern of the world, but according to the pattern created by God in Jesus Christ. Husbands and wives, for instance, are *both* called to live out the relational norm of humble, servant love, even if Paul applies that norm to each of them in a unique and complementary mode.

As we have already observed, this pattern of life is one which reflects the life of the Trinity. The Trinity is an eternal community of self-giving love, or to take a step further (into admittedly more speculative territory), as a community of mutual submission. The passage from Philippians famously uses the verb *kenao*, or *to empty*, from which we get the theological word *kenosis*. The passage expresses the idea that Christ emptied himself or poured himself out. That has led to many theological discussions regarding what exactly such *emptying* means, since Christ never ceased to be divine. At the very least, though, it demonstrates a laying down of divine rights. The one who deserves to sit at the Father's right hand, and who even now is enthroned there, came to the earth in utter humility, taking on human form with all its weaknesses and limitations, and died in the manner of a despised criminal. To conventional wisdom, this seems like an utterly un-godlike thing to do. (Muslims, for instance, who deny that Jesus was anything more than a great prophet, reject the idea that God would so much as allow one of his beloved servants do such a thing, let alone do it himself in human flesh.)[3] But Christians ponder the mystery according to which God was never more God-like than when he hung powerless and despised upon the cross. That is at least part of the meaning of the simple but profound claim that "God is love." There on the cross, the lowest pit of human shame and suffering mysteriously coincided with the shining pinnacle of divine glory.

This invites us to consider the possibility that there is an element of self-emptying love which eternally flows between the persons of the Trinity. We can imagine the trinitarian communion as a continual dance of giving-and-receiving, or perhaps (by very dim analogy, of course) like a three-way fountain in which each one is constantly pouring itself out into the others while being filled by them.[4]

In any case, whatever the reality is for the inner life of God which lies so far beyond the grasp of our knowledge, we have seen how God's very act of creation has a self-giving quality to it; a quality made fully manifest when God came to earth in human flesh and went to the cross. That is the God in whose image we have been created, and the savior in whose likeness we are being redeemed. Therefore, that is the kind of relational life to which

---

3. See Qureshi, *Seeking Allah, Finding Jesus*, 146–54.

4. Theologians have sometimes described the Trinity using the word *perichoresis*, which invokes the image of a dance, or a kind of perpetual interpersonal motion.

we have been called. The church, and the family, are to be a community of kenosis; a people who wholeheartedly follow the command to "Submit to one another out of reverence for Christ."

The Logic of Rights versus the Logic of Love

This is a way of life which seems striking and scandalous from any number of angles. The teaching which Ephesians 5 presents about marriage often turns up in the debate between complementarianism (the traditional approach which affirms the normativity of male authority in the home and the church) and egalitarianism (which emphasizes gender equality in matters of authority). Insofar as the argument is about who has the right to authority and how much, both sides miss the point. Traditional views on gender roles often appeal to a sense of rights which are enshrined in the natural order of things: "Men, it is your right to rule. Women, it is your responsibility to cede men this right." Ephesians 5 says nothing of the sort. It calls believers, men and women together, to eagerly lay down their rights for the sake of loving service for one another. On the other hand, arguments for egalitarianism often say things like "Women, you have the right to absolute equality with men. Always stand up for that right." We should all agree that women and men are equal, such that all male chauvinism and privilege should be opposed. But again, the ethos of personal rights has a limited place (yes, a place, but a limited one) in the Christian worldview. Our life together is not to be marked by an effort to demand our rights, but an eagerness to lay them down and serve one another.

Of course, rights have an important role in our common life together in the world, particularly because of the fallen condition. They are a necessary safeguard against all kinds of evil, injustice, and abuse. To that extent they are vitally important. But they do not constitute the ultimate basis on which we are to live together as Christians. We think about how Jesus laid down his rights, and taught us to do the same. He taught us that "The rulers of the Gentiles lord it over them, and their high officials exercise authority over them. Not so with you. Instead, whoever wants to become great among you must be your servant, and whoever wants to be first must be your slave—just as the Son of Man did not come to be served, but to serve, and to give his life as a ransom for many" (Matt 20:25-28). He also taught his followers to turn the other cheek, give away their shirt when their cloak was demanded, and to go the second mile (Matt 5:38-42). Our relationships are not ultimately to be lived out on the basis of rights, which, while important as social safeguards in a fallen world, do not represent God's ideal as presented in Jesus Christ.

Both traditional patriarchalism and modern egalitarianism function on a basis of rights, whether a presumed natural right of the male to rule the female, or the right to insist on equal treatment. Between the two, I would argue that the latter is the better system insofar as it safeguards against the rampant abuse of power, but neither represent the way which Jesus has modeled. This is the way of self-giving, the way of laying down our rights for others, the way of servitude, the way of the cross. The first will be last and the last will be first. Those who want to lead should serve. If we compete with one another, it should be to outdo each other in humble service.

This is a scandal to both traditional and progressive impulses. Christians should resist the dual temptations of modern democratic egalitarianism and Christianized patriarchy. We must not be fooled into thinking that these are the only possible options. The former is problematic not because it promotes equality, but because it does so on the ultimately humanistic basis of personal rights rather than Christlike love. It also can lead toward a false kind of equality which flattens out all differences. That goes against the grain of God's church (and reality itself), which, as we saw previously, exists at the intersection of unity and diversity. God's intention for human fellowship is not a great homogenization in the name of social equality, but a society of love created by the union of distinct and diverse persons.

But the latter (Christianized patriarchy) is problematic for the same reason that slavery is; particularly the form of slavery which was practiced in the American South. Slavery and male domination are both vivid examples of power gone wrong. They belong to the category of the "realms, authorities, powers, and dominions" which the kingdom of God absolutely opposes. Like oil and water, they do not mix. While Paul may have not confronted these worldly power structures head on, his call to make servant love the foundation of the church's life together inevitably subverted them. The relational norms of God's people lead us not toward the reclamation of worldly power structures, but rather toward Christian practices and communities marked by self-giving love and mutual servitude, in which the full humanity of all as God's image bearers is recognized and lived out.

We notice here that Paul's instruction leads toward the dismantling of power structures like slavery and male domination from the inside-out rather than from the top-down. They are undermined by the formation of a new kind of person. This makes sense when we remember another concept we have already discussed: the contrast between *power-for* and *power-against*. The social norm which Christians embrace is the use of power in the service of love. This informs the logic by which we fight our battles. The characteristic posture of the Christian citizen is not that of an angry activist raging against the powers-that-be, but rather that of a loving servant who subverts those powers precisely by a refusal to be manipulated by them. Again, Martin Luther King Jr. is exemplary here in his practice of nonviolent resistance.

That Paul encourages women, children, and slaves to embrace a submissive attitude is a scandal to modern sensibilities. But he did so for a radical reason which would also have scandalized people of his own time: not to endorse the status quo but to glorify God in the world. He persistently frames the responsibility of women, children, and slaves as a matter of their relationship to God, not something owed to human beings. Even more scandalous is his instruction to husbands, parents, and masters, which consistently points them in the direction of caring, servant love rather than affirming a social status as "top dog."

Conclusion

The subject matter of this passage brings us face-to-face with all kinds of challenging and controversial issues in today's world, such as gender relations and the power dynamics between different groups and classes of people. As Christians, these issues cannot be ignored, nor can their complexity be dismissed through a false simplicity.

While this presents us with daunting challenges, we find encouragement in the fact that the heart of all these issues, complex as they may be, can be faced with a basic attitude which is quite simple (although also difficult): treat the other people with whom we live and work with humble, loving servitude. Of course, the exact shape such servitude takes depends on the particularities of the relationship. Parents should indeed treat their toddlers with servant love, but this, of course, cannot mean abdicating authority and letting them do whatever they want. It means that the ultimate good of the persons in question—whatever their age, gender, or workplace rank—is regarded as a priority. It means that we value these people more highly than our own pride and ambition. We resist the temptations of pride, power, and control in all their forms. We live by the code that people matter more than personal agendas.

Here, near the end of Paul's short letter to the Ephesians, we have seen perhaps most clearly what his vision for God-glorifying human existence looks like in practice. God's plan to manifest his grace and glory, which has been enacted by Jesus Christ, takes its shape in the everyday relationships of ordinary people who are being transformed into his likeness. Ephesians presents a vision no less lofty than the reunification of all things, through Jesus Christ and for the eternal glory of God. Yet this great vision plays out in the humblest of places: words and actions of love, kindness, and servitude, freely exchanged by people in their homes and workplaces.

As a plan to turn the world upside-down (or perhaps right-side-up again), it is almost embarrassingly simple. In the context of our world's controversies, driven by both the pride of power and the pride of outrage against the powerful, it is scandalous. But for those who are being saved, it is the very power and wisdom of God. It is a power which we have the opportunity to exercise daily as we use our strength in service for one another. It is a wisdom which is incarnate in simple acts of love and mercy—the kind which do not always make sense according to the common-sense of the world.

In short, the meaning of human existence, when comprehended in the light of Jesus Christ, is not a thing far beyond our reach. It is as near to us as the nearest human person. It is as close as our wife or our husband, our child or our parent, our coworker, the person sitting next to us on the pew—or even the stranger on the airplane seat. Wherever we find ourselves, we are never far from someone we can humbly serve in the self-giving love of Jesus Christ. To do so is to grasp God's hand and take our place in the partnership for which we were created: loving fellowship with God and one another.

Father, we thank you for the love in which you have created and redeemed the world. We thank you that this love is not only a reality for us to know, but one in which you have called us to participate. You have so freely and graciously given yourself to us, even pouring out your blood on the cross. Your love has given us life. Therefore may we truly live in it, as we share with others that which we have so abundantly received from you. May your love live not only in our hearts, but in every relationship. May our churches, homes, and workplaces become habitats of this love. Form us, Heavenly Father, by your Holy Spirit, after the image of your Son, that in our life together we may know the more of your love, and that your love may become more fully known in all the world. Amen.

10

The Scandal of Warfare

Paraphrase: Ephesians 6:10-24

FINALLY, BE STRONG IN the Lord. May his power be your strength! Put on his armor for strength, so that you will be able to stand against all the clever schemes of the evil one. For our battle is not against flesh-and-blood people, but against the rulers, authorities, and cosmic powers of this present age of darkness—against the spiritual forces in the heavenly places. Therefore, put on the full armor of God, so that you will be able to stand strong against those forces when they press their attack. Stand your ground. Wear truth like a belt around your waist, and righteousness like a bulletproof vest. Be as fleet-footed as a warrior in your proclamation of the gospel of peace. Carry faith like a shield to fend off the flaming missiles of the evil one. Wear your salvation like a helmet, and wield the word of God like a Spirit-given sword.

In addition, arm yourself continually with prayer in the Spirit. Be attentive and persistent in praying on behalf of God's holy people. In this way, pray also for me, so that I may boldly speak the message God gives me to reveal the mystery of the gospel. It is for this gospel, of which I am an ambassador, that I am in chains. Pray that I will declare it as I should: with boldness.

I am sending Tychicus to you so that he can fill you in on how I am and what I am doing. He is a dear friend and a faithful servant of the Lord. He will give you a report from us and give you much encouragement.

Peace, love, and faith be to all of you, from God the Father and the Lord Jesus Christ. Grace be with all of you whose love for him is undying.

The Scandal of Warfare

In the previous passage, we explored the idea that self-giving, servant love should be present in all the relationships of God's people. The attentive reader and critical thinker must suspect all along that there must be some other side of the coin to this. Not that a Christian is called to be anything less than loving, but we sense that there is also more to it than that. Life in our world is challenging and complex. Here love covers a multitude of sins, but is it the only thing we have to think about? Are there not also battles to be fought?

That brings us to the next and final passage in Ephesians. The Christian life is one of love, but it is also lived in the midst of a battlefield. After telling his audience to care for one another with humble love and respect in all their various relationships, Paul concludes by giving them instructions on how to suit up for battle. Are Christians to be lovers, or fighters? The answer appears to be "both." No doubt this involves a challenging tension, but when we understand the nature of the battle, the duality begins to make much more sense than we might first suppose.

It helps, as usual, to take in the wider view. This is not the first time in Ephesians that Paul has mentioned the spiritual battle in which God's people are involved. In 1:20–22, Paul describes how Jesus Christ has ascended to rule in power "far above all rule and authority, power and dominion." In 2:1–3, Paul describes how all of us have naturally been enemies of God, following "the ways of this world and of the ruler of the kingdom of the air, the spirit who is now at work in those who are disobedient." But through Christ we have been redeemed, "raised up with Christ and seated with him in the heavenly realms (2:5), so that God's purpose will be accomplished: that "the manifold wisdom of God should be made known to the rulers and authorities in the heavenly realms (3:10–11). In short, Paul has all along been showing how human life is lived in the midst of a battlefield between the powers of God and those of an enemy, and that we must serve one or the other.

The Divine Warrior

This idea of God as a warrior is not, of course, a new one at this point in Scripture. The whole Bible is a narrative depicting God engaged in a battle against forces of evil. Often throughout the Old Testament God fights against those who threaten his chosen people. Sometimes he even fights against his own people, when they persistently rebel against him. That, of course, is a very sobering picture. But in all cases, it is the goodness and faithfulness of God which is proved. God can be counted on to oppose all evil and to be faithful to the promises he has made. Even when he takes up arms against his own would-be people, it is because they have rebelled against his covenant. God never betrays his people, but neither does God betray himself. When God fights, it is always on the side of truth, justice, righteousness, and love.

There's something admittedly a bit odd about the idea of an omnipotent God fighting battles within the world of his creation. We might easily imagine local tribal deities fighting against each other, or pantheons of pagan gods squabbling among themselves. Or it might make sense to think in terms of ancient Zoroastrian or Manichean religions which believed in a good God locked in an eternal struggle with a coeternal but evil counterpart. But these conceptions are all foreign to the faith of Scripture, where there is one creator God alone who is in charge of the universe. What kind of battle can such a God fight? Can God make war against any created power, any more than a man can make war against an earthworm crawling before him on the ground? How can there even be a contest?

A human—or even all of them together—is weaker in comparison to God than any worm is to a man. Yet to God, we mean much more. We are created as bearers of a glorious purpose; as bearers of divine love in relationship to God and others. And with this purpose comes power. Not absolute power, yet a delegated power great enough to have catastrophic consequences when misused in the world. God has also, it seems, delegated powers to spiritual beings, some of whom are also in rebellion against him. In this way, we know the nature of the battle: it is not like a war between two rival nations; not even nations of greatly different power. It is a civil war; a rebellion and an uprising of creatures against their creator. Against him, humans and spiritual beings have formed allegiances and solidarities of hideous strength—yet nothing which a single word of God could not tear down in an instant.[1]

Of course, this raises all kinds of difficult questions; namely what we call the problem of evil: if God is all that powerful, and all that good, why hasn't he spoken that word yet? Why hasn't he laid waste all the hosts of evil and plunged them into blackest darkness? Here we encounter the surprising answer: God has indeed spoken his word. The word is that which "was

---

1. As Martin Luther put it in his great hymn "A Mighty Fortress Is Our God," "A single word shall fell him."

with God in the beginning." It is his Son, Jesus Christ. God's word, which he has uttered against all his enemies, is *mercy*. The problem of evil cannot, perhaps, be so simply dealt with, but that accounts for at least a great part of the matter.[2] The reason evil still endures (or at least part of the reason) is because God is merciful enough to give the wicked ample opportunity to repent. If God were to obliterate all evil this instant, it would mean certain death, even for you and me. That end will eventually come for those who persist in rebellion, as God has promised. But in the meantime, God is patient. This present age is a kind of blessed contradiction, as a time in which it is possible to be in rebellion against the giver of life and yet still draw breath. It is a contradiction sustained, for a season, by God's patient love.

Now we have an even better sense of the kind war God is fighting. The battle lines are drawn out, as it were, between the hosts of heaven and the legions of hell. To be a sentient creature in this universe is to be on one side of the line or the other—and all of us as humans are, by nature, on the wrong side of the line. But God does not fight like an ordinary general. Although he has the power to end the battle any time, he is now simply holding his enemies at bay, and this gives him occasion to go about the work in which he is most passionately invested. God is like a general who sneaks across the battle line and into the enemy camp, like a thief by night, to plead with them one at a time to come over to his side. The day of battle is coming, when arrows will darken the sky, swords will flash like a thousand stars, and God's victory will be complete. But until that day, God is rescuing all he can—all who will respond to him in faith. That is where the battle rages now: in the hearts of men and women, whose pardon has already been paid for by God's own self-sacrifice through the cross.

That is why Paul writes that "our battle is not against flesh and blood." God's war is not against human persons, but for them. A day is coming

---

2. This kind of response to the problem of evil will be seen by many to be inadequate—which, like all answers, it doubtlessly is. But one of the main reasons why such an answer might be rejected is because of a presupposition about the problem of evil; namely, that the greatest evils are those of pain, suffering, and death. My presupposition is different: that the greatest evil is rebellion against God and eternal separation from him. Pain and suffering are evils, but only relative evils. They can even function as relative goods insofar as they are symptoms which alert us to the true nature of the world's fallen state. Many ways of formulating the problem of evil lay the blame on God for permitting so much pain and suffering in the world. To do so is to complain that God hasn't eradicated the symptoms of our condition even while he has already provided the cure in Jesus Christ. As modern people we are habitually far too concerned about our earthly comfort. God in his love is more concerned about our eternal condition.

for final judgement, but until that day, God seeks to extract sinful humans from the system of evil in which they are complicit but are also victims and captives.³ While God is justified in looking at all people as his enemies awaiting destruction, in his love he chooses to view them as objects of his gracious redemptive initiative; as potential bearers of divine glory.

The Enemy

But if "flesh and blood" are not to be regarded as the true enemy, then who is? Paul tells us directly, if still rather mysteriously: "The rulers, authorities, and cosmic powers of this present age of darkness—against the spiritual forces in the heavenly places." It would seem that Paul has in mind here demonic forces. It can be challenging, especially for twenty-first-century Western people, to know how to make proper sense of this. Most people nowadays are not eager to blame the troubles of the world on evil spirits. To do so may seem superstitious, harkening back to times when problems in life were solved by hiring witch doctors—or burning witches.

But such caricatures will not do. Christians do not claim that there are mischievous little devils crouching behind every bush, but that there are in fact demonic forces—forces of evil and opposition to God—which are at work in the world and which wage war against God's people. There are two levels at which we can recognize that such demonic power in the world is not only conceivable, but in fact hard to miss: the enemy within, and the enemy without.

The Enemy Within

We have already noted how all of us, by nature, are both the victims of evil and complicit with it. That is the human condition, from which God in his mercy desires to redeem us. When we ask the question "What's wrong with

---

3. Here we think of the common statement that "God loves the sinner but hates the sin." This is true, but not in a way that allows us to take it for granted or make it an axiom about the nature of sin. It is not natural to differentiate sinners and their sin. To an extent, we are what we do and we do what we are. It is only by the power of the cross that sinners can be separated from their sin at all. We can think of the cross as a scalpel in the hand of an almighty surgeon, by which he cuts sin from sinner as cancer from flesh. The gospel is the good news that God in Christ treats us according to his righteousness rather than our sin, having taken the sin on himself.

The Scandal of Warfare

the world?" our answer must at least include the statement "I am."[4] One of the more sobering facts of life is how quickly, when honestly examining ourselves, we find all sorts of weakness, pride, and selfishness—frequently the very things which we are so disposed to abhor in others. Not for a moment should we abdicate personal responsibility for these things with a perfunctory excuse that "the devil made me do it." Yet that influence is not to be laughed at. The truth is not so much that demons make us do bad things, but rather that it is in our nature to quietly agree with them and their values; namely the inclination to be a self-centered person in a God-centered universe.

There is no better picture of the influences and allegiances between the human heart and the powers of evil than that which C. S. Lewis has sketched in *The Screwtape Letters*.[5] Of course the whole scenario of the book—a high-ranking demon writing letters of advice to a bumbling junior tempter—is fanciful and even quite darkly comic. But the contents of these letters brilliantly expose the psychology of evil, alerting us to the reality that even our little, everyday quarrels may be the mask of a spiritual battle imperiling our souls. As Lewis reminds us, we do not need to look far at all to see the work of the evil one; perhaps not any further than the thoughts of our own heart. To that extent, spiritual warfare consists of the daily spiritual discipline of examining ourselves and giving ourselves over, once again, to God.

The Enemy Without

The power of the evil one is not only at work within our hearts, but also in the public arena. Throughout the New Testament, we frequently find this implied in terms such as "the world" and "the flesh," which often have in view the concept of sin and evil as a whole realm or a systemic network of wills and activities existing and operating in opposition to God. In other words, sin is not only individual; it's also corporate and systemic. If individual people sometimes find themselves operating in cooperation with the powers in rebellion against God, certainly larger social structures and solidarities can and do fall into such sinister allegiances.

One of the great dangers of such patterns of evil is that as prevalent as they are, they can be difficult to recognize precisely because of their

---

4. This reply has been attributed to G. K. Chesterton.
5. Lewis, *Screwtape Letters*.

familiarity. Systemic evil can be as invisible to us as water is to a fish. Perhaps the best way to illustrate it is with a sketch of a hypothetical person who is impacted by the powers of evil at several different points.

Sarah, as we shall call her, is a struggling young mother. She has two young children, but is separated from their father. She is hardworking and responsible, but finds herself inextricably enmeshed in poverty. She works more than full-time, but can only find minimum-wage jobs which do not adequately support her and her children. Numerous complications surround this struggle. Affording childcare is difficult for her. When she can't afford day care, she has to miss work to care for her children. This has led to her losing her job several times. Although she is otherwise a good worker, her work record always appears poor on paper and keeps her from getting better jobs or promotions. One of her children also suffers from some moderate medical issues which has led to financial problems, especially because of her inconsistent work. She seems to continually find herself caught between making too much money to be on affordable health-care programs, yet not enough to be able to buy insurance herself or pay for expenses out-of-pocket. She finds herself continuously trying to navigate the labyrinthian world of affordable housing. It also seems to be a factor that Sarah is a person of color. Although few of the people with whom Sarah deals are explicitly racist, it seems that she keeps hitting invisible walls that are difficult to explain any other way.

Recently, Sarah was sexually assaulted by her former manager at work. She pressed charges, but he claimed, with the help of his lawyer, that their encounter was consensual. Sarah could not afford to hire a lawyer, and it quickly became obvious to her that it was easier just to drop the charges than to persevere in fighting a complex legal battle herself. She quit her job since she obviously did not feel safe around her manager. Then she discovered that she was pregnant from the encounter. In desperation, she chose to have an abortion, not knowing how she would care for another child and feeling unable to emotionally deal with having a child under the circumstances. In addition, she felt sure that she could not afford a hospital childbirth, whereas an abortion could be funded. Sarah confided about these events to a member of her church, who then spread the news that she had had an abortion. Soon she found herself shunned and ostracized by other members of the church. Sarah did not have a long-term background in church attendance, nor was she confident or well-grounded in her Christian faith. Without any other community of believers to give her a more well-rounded view of things, she concluded that Christians could not be trusted, and that Christian belief was not for her.

Notice all the influences and powers which have destructively converged on Sarah. Numerous individuals—and Sarah herself—sin throughout her story, but all the individual sins add up into something that is greater and more terrible than their sum. As a person of color, she is born into a society with both lingering undercurrents of racism and certain systemic disadvantages based on multigenerational patterns. Various individuals with mildly—even unconsciously—racist attitudes have disadvantaged her at key moments in her life. She is enmeshed in an economic system which is designed for the benefit of corporate wealth and the buying habits of middle-class consumers rather than the real good of individuals and families. This makes it hard for her both to afford key goods (especially medical care) and to get a job for which she is well-paid, or one which gives voice to her real talents and abilities, and which views her as a person rather than a cog in a machine. She has also encountered the de-facto law of the legal world in which all are equal before the law, except for those who cannot afford good lawyers—as well as the age-old principle that in matters of disputed claims, the tie goes to the powerful. She is the victim of the breakdown of the family, since her status as a single parent is one of the biggest factors making life difficult for her at every turn. Many of her own mistakes led to this, but blame also lies at the feet of the father of children. More to the point, she has grown up in a world which has gone far in the direction of jettisoning the very ideas of a stable home and relational commitment, which are essential foundations for human flourishing. She also lives in a world which has not adequately taught the value of life and has made the aborting of her child a choice which is, for her, easier and even more attractive than the alternatives. For Sarah, access to abortion was made easier than any means of carrying or delivering her child. Finally, Sarah found herself part of a church community which refused to be the church for her, pushing her away precisely at the time when she most needed faithful support and love. She became isolated not only from supportive community, but also from God himself.

The purpose of this story has not been to indulge in pernicious stereotypes, but rather, through perhaps some exaggeration, to illuminate unfortunate truths. I am not aware of anyone who has experienced all of Sarah's woes, but these kinds of things sadly happen all the time, to multitudes of persons, and in endless variations. Nor is the point to exonerate Sarah of all blame. She made many mistakes along the way—but mistakes whose consequences are far milder for those who are fortunate enough to belong to the right set. In addition to being horribly sinned against, she has made (like all of us) some mistakes for which she needs to take responsibility. Yet, we also need to give just consideration to the fact that she grew up in a world which never taught her how to live and then heaped punishment after punishment upon her when she made mistakes as a result.

We also note the political factors at work through all of this. Forces which come from many different places in society, both from so-called "liberal" and "conservative" directions, seem actually to be in sinister league with each other when it comes to the destruction of human persons. Conservatives blame liberals for the injustice of abortion against the unborn and for the destruction of family values. Liberals blame conservatives for failure to take responsibility for issues of social, racial, and economic justice. Both sides blame each other while quietly, if unintentionally, cooperating in the net effect of the proliferation of evil and injustice.

This is a portrait—really just a minute glimpse—of the schemes in which people are ensnared at the hands of "the rulers, authorities, and cosmic powers of this present age of darkness." Again, that is no denial of personal responsibility—sin is a crime of which we are both the victims and the perpetrators—but here we see that evil in the world is horribly greater than mere random acts of individual people. Those acts frequently turn out to be like mosaic stones in master-fresco of destructive, demonic force.

Servants of the Divine Warrior

This is horribly discouraging, but for knowledge of God's (already but not yet) victory over the powers of evil through Jesus Christ. God's power—the creative power of love—has spoken definitively through the cross, and we know that it will have the final word. In the meantime, God is creating his own mosaic, made of people in his image after the pattern of Christ. Here again, the small acts of God's people are together, through the unifying work of the Holy Spirit, greater than the sum of their individual effects. Through the presence of people in the world who really belong to Christ and who stand against the devil's schemes, God is building his kingdom.

Now we see more clearly what it means to be an agent of the divine warrior. As we said earlier, God is a paradoxical kind of warrior who crosses over the enemy lines to wrestle with the hearts of men and women—even as he once wrestled with a man named Jacob and changed his name to Israel (which means *he struggles with God*). Christians are those in the enemy camp who have responded in faith to God's gracious initiative and have become his allies. In terms of allegiance and identity, we have come over to God's side. But the challenge and the opportunity of the Christian life lies in the fact that we still physically reside in enemy territory. We still live on an earth which is fractured by the fall and swayed by the schemes of the evil one. The church (to borrow an image from C. S. Lewis) is like a secret resistance army living in enemy-occupied territory, awaiting the great invasion which is yet to take place.[6]

But our neighbors who do not yet belong to God's army are not to be regarded as the enemy. Our struggle is not against flesh and blood. We are called to see all people the way God sees them: as beloved objects of his redemptive purposes. Therefore we partner with God in his work behind enemy lines, cooperating with him in the redemption of ourselves and our fellow human beings.

But this, of course, is a highly subversive activity. We are, after the pattern of God himself, seeking to undermine the networks of evil in which people are ensnared. The Christian life and calling puts us decidedly at odds against the reigning world orders, and that makes us, from the world's perspective, a scandalous people.

As we read here at the end of Ephesians, God has outfitted us for our mission. He has armed us defensively against the works of the enemy (both within and without), and has also equipped us for the work of liberating and redeeming our fellow captives. Paul uses a suit of armor as a vivid object lesson to describe this. Although surely each of these items of the warrior's arsenal deserves great attention, we will only think about each briefly, with attention to its importance in the battle against evil in which we find ourselves.

Truth

Jesus once referred to Satan as "the father of lies" (John 8:44). He also said that "The truth will set you free" (John 8:32). Deception and falsehood are key devices of evil. Servants of the divine warrior are those who speak the truth in love, and more than that, are personally rooted in the truth themselves. One of the first and most important tasks in the opposition

---

6. Lewis, *Mere Christianity*, 51.

of evil is simply naming it; calling it out for what it is. This involves both the personal and compassionate work of giving truth and clarity to those who are caught in patterns of destruction, and also the courageous work of "speaking truth to power." Evil thrives in the dark. Our task is help shed the light of truth on it. As Paul said earlier in Ephesians 5:11, "Have nothing to do with the fruitless deeds of darkness, but rather expose them."

Righteousness

Paul tells his audience to put on the breastplate of righteousness. Perhaps it is significant that a breastplate (or today's equivalent, the bulletproof vest), has a purely defensive purpose. If we follow through with Paul's analogy, we are led to think of righteousness not as a weapon by which we win offensive battles in the world, but something essentially protective. To be righteous is not to bring a particular agenda to bear on the rest of the world, but to inhabit the world as a particular kind of person. In other words, righteousness is not inherently an attempt to change the world, but merely to take responsibility for oneself before God as we live within it. The paradox is that by doing so, one changes the world. A person who inhabits the righteousness of God by faith (for there is no other way to be righteous) is not on an active mission to go forth and destroy all evil. But he or she inevitably responds righteously in the face of whatever is encountered in the world. To be such a person is to be one whom evil cannot infect, nor reflect off of so as to damage others. God's people, who are righteous (and this does not mean sinless), are therefore like antibodies against evil in the world. Or, to use a picture presented by Jesus, they are like salt, a small pinch of which works its way through the whole recipe and transforms it.

The Gospel of Peace

As we saw in Ephesians 2:11–22, the gospel (the good news) is all about peace: peace with God, and peace with one another. In particular, we saw how the work of Christ creates a new social solidarity that tears down the primacy of old identities which divide people. Here we come to the heart of a Christian response to evil. All evil ultimately derives from the condition of a broken relationship with God, and it leads to the brokenness of all other relationships. Only through the gospel are these unions restored.

As it turns out, much evil in the world is manifest in those false solidarities which demand the allegiance which belongs to God alone and which divide people into prideful polarities between "us" and "them." That accounts for much of the psychology of evil within the individual human heart, which views other people through a lens of pride. It also accounts for many great social evils, such as those perpetrated by boastful empires and other solidarities of the strong.

But the gospel is God's weapon against all this. It disarms the human pride which separates us from God and each other and provides the forgiveness which alone can restore us to the fellowship for which we were created. The gospel is God's nail-pierced hand outstretched toward the world. To be a Christian is to grasp his hand, not only for our own redemption, but for the joining of his work of redeeming others.

Faith

In Paul's vivid analogy, we take up the shield of faith to fend off the flaming arrows of the evil one. Again, this points toward a defensive rather than offensive posture. There are probably many levels on which we can think about how faith defends us from evil. Faith, defined as belief in the truth, protects us from false teachings. Defined as personal trust in God, faith moors our life to his and gives us a stable foundation for our identity and existence. Another helpful way to define faith (as suggested by Hebrews 11) is living faithfully in light of a future which is already real in Jesus Christ but which is not yet visible on earth. In other words, faith means living as a *new creation* person in the midst of the *old creation* world; as members of God's company even while inhabiting the enemy camp. It means that our membership in the kingdom of God defines our identity and our way of life rather than the norms of the present age. That is a great defense against the strategies of evil, which so often gain their power by claiming to define the identities of those they oppress, as well as those of the oppressors. There is a great power of resistance against evil simply in knowing who we are. To live out our allegiance to the kingdom of God in the midst of this world is an act of subversive love. Evil cannot shake those who have utter confidence that God will have the final word.

Salvation

The "helmet of salvation" (again a defensive piece of armor) seems like a more general item. *Salvation* seems to cover all the Christian life like an umbrella. Not that every part of the Christian life is equated with salvation, but it is the basic condition or source from which everything flows. The basic fact of life for God's people is that God has (already but not yet) saved them both *from* sin and death and hell, and saved them *for* blessed fellowship with God and one another, through which the goodness and glory of God is reflected, manifested, and enjoyed. In that sense, salvation has to do with everything in the Christian life, and in fact, every legitimate thing in the universe.

Thinking of our salvation as defensive armor against evil makes obvious sense to the degree that our salvation is simply the reality that God has rescued us (again, already but not yet) from the evil of rebellion against God and eternal separation from him. In terms of Paul's analogy, we could think of "putting on the helmet of salvation" as grasping that which God has done for us through Christ and being mindful of the security we have in him, such that the powers of evil can do nothing to separate us from the love of God (see Romans 8:38–39).

Scripture

In Paul's object lesson, Scripture is the primary offensive weapon against evil. We can see this exemplified by Jesus himself. When confronted in the wilderness by Satan, Jesus responded with Scripture. This is not the end of that story either: it comes to a thunderous conclusion in the book of Revelation, where the Lamb who was slain brings the devil and all the powers of evil to their final defeat. Christ's chief weapon here is God's word, depicted in Revelation's vivid imagery as a "sharp, double-edged sword" coming from his mouth (Rev 1.16). The strongest weapon against the father of lies is the truth which God has spoken in the Scriptures and his son.

The comparison between Scripture and a sword is also used to powerful effect in Hebrews 4:12–13. Here, instead of emphasizing our use of Scripture to change and convict the world, the author of Hebrews highlights God's use of Scripture to change and convict us. It's important to keep that in perspective. Evil is ultimately conquered, convicted, and destroyed by the truth of God. But we need to receive and inhabit God's truth—and therefore be changed by it—before we wield it against the world. Perhaps this is all another way of saying what Jesus so pithily described when he taught his followers to take the logs out of their own eye first, and only then turn to help their neighbors remove the specks of sawdust from their own.

But this disclaimer should not take the sharp edge off the essential point: that our defense and opposition to the powers of evil come through living in the world in light of God's truth which he has spoken to us. To do this, we ourselves need to rightly receive and understand God's word, and then respond in the obedience which is by faith. We see how Paul's extended analogy of "the armor of God" has come full circle and ended where it began: with an emphasis on being rooted firmly in the truth and faithfully enacting it in the world through our words and actions.

Prayer

Although Paul has finished his armor analogy, there is another piece of weaponry that remains: prayer. Considering prayer as a weapon against evil calls us to confront two opposite and pervasive assumptions. The first is that prayer is the only weapon against evil, and the second is that prayer is mere sentimentality and a waste of time. The first erroneous assumption is that after praying about an occurrence of evil or suffering in the world, we think our work is done. The second is that we neglect the work of prayer altogether. In response to tragedy, we must go beyond perfunctory "thoughts and prayers." At the same time, we must not neglect the odd but glorious duty God has laid upon us to plead with him on behalf of the world. Paul, as an ambassador of the gospel, which is the very power of God, appeals to the prayers of his audience in order to confront the powers of evil which have imprisoned him. Paul apparently understands that God has surprisingly delegated some of his power to his people, so that the battle against God's cosmic enemies might be fought partly in and through us—whether we are on our feet or our knees.

Conclusion

Here at the end, we can pull some of the strands of this chapter together. Our world is a battlefield between God and the powers of evil. God is a warrior and we who believe are conscripted into his army. But God is a warrior of mercy and we are an army of redemption. We join God in fighting against the powers and principalities which weave their webs of deception and destruction in the world. We fight against these spiritual powers, on behalf of the people who are held captive by them. This is a war which is waged both in the public arena, where many injustices flourish, and in our own hearts. We fight the deception by living in the truth. We battle the destruction at work in old creation by living in the power of the new.

Earlier we sketched a hypothetical person oppressed by the various structures of evil in the world, the woman we called "Sarah." Sarah may be hypothetical, but she is nonetheless very real. Sarah lives down the street. She's a member of our family. She sits next to us in the church pew. Many of us, whatever our race or gender, see her when we look in the mirror. She is the object of Satan's destructive schemes, God's sacrificial love, and our redeeming work. The cosmic battle plays out in our daily encounters with Sarah.

God has equipped us with the crucial equipment for these encounters. He has outfitted his people as warriors of love—and our love of the good must entail a hatred of evil. But God's strategy is surprising. It is, in its current stage, one of patience and subversion, not a frontal assault. We fight by standing in the truth which God has spoken in his word, being identified by the salvation in which we partake by faith. In part, this means that we fight by the refusal to be a conduit of evil. We are a nonconductive piece of wire in the world's weblike circuitry of evil. We are those who can say to evil, in all its malicious patterns of cause-and-effect, "The buck stops here." Yet this by no means calls us to be merely passive. While we refuse to be conduits of evil, we are eager conductors of the loving power of God: the power which created the world, and which—with the participation of God's people—will redeem it.

We praise you, Father, for your strength. We praise you for the great power which is yours alone, yet we thank you that you have also equipped us with your power as we face your enemies in this age. We thank you that you have not left us alone in the midst of the destructive forces which roam the earth, but that you, in your almighty grace, have made us bearers of your power and agents of your love.

So Lord, as your people, we look to you. Ground us in your truth, that we may stand against deceptions. Draw us into your righteousness, that we may resist evil. Invigorate us with zeal for your gospel, that we may speak your love for a world in need. Fill us with faith, that we may inhabit your faithfulness. Assure us of your salvation, that we may know we are yours. Arm us with your word of truth, that we may triumph over the evil one.

Give us your eyes to see the world, O Lord, your love to feel its pain, and your strength to face its injustices. Give us your heart for the world, that prayers for your saints and the world's wounded may ever be upon our lips.

To you be the praise and the glory, O Lord: for the gifts of peace, love, and faith, given in the abundance of grace which is ours in Christ Jesus, whom we love and whose love for us is undying. For his sake and in the power of your Spirit we pray. Amen!

Conclusion

The Meaning of Christianity and the Scandal of Christian Existence

WE CANNOT LIVE WELL without a compelling vision of what life is all about. Every human civilization—and even every human individual—seeks refuge within a story that accounts for the reality we behold and accords us a meaningful place in it. For many of us, this vision of reality is more implicit than explicit. We may not have thought much about it at all on a conscious level. But it is there: in the form of memories which tether us to past events we consider meaningful and formative; in the form of groups with which we identify; in the form of relationships which give us joy; in the form of the activities which comprise our priorities; in the form of heroes who command our admiration; in the form of our sorrows or outrages evoked by world events; in the form of present fears and future hopes. These are all informed, whether consciously or otherwise, by underlying assumptions about the nature of reality; about what is good, true, and beautiful; about what is worthy of our value, our understanding, and our desire.

Too often, however, we ascribe value to things without considering whether they are good, assume understanding without a proper pursuit of the truth, and bestow our craving admirations without regard for ultimate worth. Ours is a civilization that delights to dwell on the shimmering surface of things; we have no time for the depths. We all assume a vision of the meaning of life, but we would rather not be troubled by who or what is projecting that vision before our eyes. We do not care if our delights are hollow and fleeting, so long as they are cheap, abundant, and delivered on time. We live in a world which tells us in a thousand voices what we want and then promises to gratify those desires with the push of a button. And yet we are not satisfied. We do not know what we really want. We know that there must be more to life. And yet "more" is offered to us in so many shining packages. The truth, goodness, and beauty we seek get lost so quickly amid the clutter of our frantic world.

And there are powers in the world who benefit from keeping it that way. We know their voices: "Don't wait—the offer ends soon! Buy now!" "Indulge yourself; you deserve it!" "Don't ask questions or seek the facts—be outraged!" "Adopt our narrative, or you are part of the problem." "You will never be good enough until you use our product." "Toe the party line, or you are a traitor." There are manipulative powerbrokers around every corner, and they all have a vision for life on sale.

That is not only a fertile ground for deception, but also for cynicism. Ours is not only the age of the bedazzled consumer, but also the jaded skeptic, who knows nothing except that he "knows better." He will have no fake happiness; only straightforward despair.

This is the gladiatorial arena in which our worldviews battle for acceptance. It is here that we cast our visions and tell our stories. We desperately want to make sense of life, and to do so, we turn not only to our myriad amusements, but also our philosophies, our politics, our religions, and they all compete for the right to explain the world. In our pluralistic age, any commitment to a particular worldview will be scandalous to someone, and Christian faith is no exception.

The Meaning of Christianity

We have said that we cannot live well without a compelling vision for the meaning of life. The Christian faith offers us this, and there is no better place to see this vision clearly than in Paul's letter to the Ephesians. Here we find a concise explanation of the meaning of Christianity within the context of a vision for the meaning of all things.

Here is the bold argument of Ephesians: God's eternal purpose has always been to create a holy people by bringing them into union with Christ and one another, in opposition to the spiritual powers at work in the world, so that through his power and by his grace, his wisdom and glory are demonstrated in them. God has chosen to manifest his eternal wisdom through finite and fallen human beings. God the almighty chose to delegate some of his ruling power to his creatures, so that they might reflect the image of his glory all the more brilliantly by serving him and one another

CONCLUSION

in the kind of self-giving love which is the eternal reality of the Trinity. We live in a world in which this loving "power-for" has been grossly misused and twisted by the hands of fallen creatures into prideful "power-against." This is a rebellion in which all humans are naturally participants, but also victims and captives of sinister forces at work in the world. Evil—the fragmentation of relationships and reality through rebellion against God—is a crime of which we are both the victims and perpetrators. But God has created a solution to the problem of evil in and through Jesus Christ, in whose suffering he has taken the brunt of the consequences on himself. The unity of all things which God purposed from the beginning has now been reasserted in Christ's death and resurrection. The center and meaning of all things, through which they have their unity of origin and purpose, is not an abstract idea, but the person of Jesus Christ, in whom God has proved himself righteous on behalf of his people. In him, God has recreated the world, and Christians are those who inhabit this present and future realm through faith. By their union with Christ, God's people stand with him at the center of all things, where they are restored to their vocation of glorifying God; that is, celebrating and showcasing his goodness, wisdom, and love. As a people who have been graciously redeemed out of their old allegiance to the powers of darkness, they now inhabit a new circle of solidarity, which creates peace by tearing down old boundaries, decentralizing all other circles, and binding God's people together in a fellowship of servant love and mutual submission out of reverence for Christ. This creates a new norm for everyday life, defined by allegiance to God's kingdom and manifested by adopting God's pattern of self-giving, servant love in all activities and relationships. God's ongoing creation of such a people is his surprising strategy for fighting the powers of evil and for establishing his loving and glorious purpose for the universe. In this way, God's people understand how the meaning of all reality (Jesus Christ) is the meaning of our everyday lives in this world.

The Scandal of Christian Existence

God looked out upon the earth and said "I see the churches, yes. But where are the Christians?"

This is not a real question of theological speculation. We are confident that God does indeed have a people on earth, and that he knows those who are his. The question is one of self-examination. It penetrates our hearts, like the question asked by Jesus: "When the Son of Man comes, will he find faith on earth?" (Luke 18:8). We know that God has a people of faith. The question is, "Am I one of them? Am I a participant in God's true church—his scandalous people?"

It will not do to settle with a report about our own church attendance. To paraphrase John the Baptist: "Produce fruit in keeping with repentance. And don't say to yourselves, *'We are members of a church.'* *For I tell you that out of these stones God can raise up churches and members of churches.* The ax is already at the root of the trees, and every tree that does not produce good fruit will be cut down and thrown into the fire" (Luke 3:7–9; emphasis added). John's actual statement is "Do not say to yourselves 'We have Abraham as our father.' For I tell you that out of these stones God can raise up children of Abraham." But I believe that there is a striking parallel between the way in which John's audience identified themselves as God's people ethnically and the way in which many modern people identify themselves as God's people institutionally. It's not that institutions are bad. They are actually necessary to most of the things we do as humans. It's just how we work. The problem is that in the larger scheme of things, they come cheap. The God who already owns the cattle on a thousand hills and the cathedrals in a thousand cities can make another church—or church member—with the snap of his fingers. What he really wants is another person who loves and obeys him—heart, soul, mind, and strength. And for that he needs our cooperation. The primary question is not whether we attend a church and are keeping sufficiently busy there (important as that may be). It is whether we are God's man or woman through-and-through; whether we are a part of that collectivity of God's-holy-people-in-Christ-through-faith. It is whether we are a member of that people who have responded to God's scandalous love and now inhabit it as it flows out into all the world. Where there is faith, hope, and love expressed through allegiance to God's kingdom and servanthood for God's creatures, there is the church God is building in the world. God really has such a people; a people who look like their Savior. The question is, "Am I a part of this people?" And if so, "Do I really live like I'm a part of them?"

Christian faith, as presented by Ephesians, is a call to embrace the humbling and spectacular privilege God has given us in Christ to partner with him in the celebration of his goodness, wisdom, and love. God has not merely invited us to behold that as a vision for life, but to embrace it as a reality of daily living; to really be the kind of person who, being redeemed

Conclusion

by God's grace for God's purposes in Christ, inhabits the true meaning of life as established by God in the creation and redemption of all things. Nor is this just a vision for individual life, but for the life of God's people, who are a society created by and for the self-giving love of God; crafted as his instrument to put his wisdom on display before the rebellious powers of the age. We must not settle for a lesser vision of Christianity than this.

Unfortunately, that is what the modern-day church has too often done, in a multitude of ways. We have the church of cultural Christianity; the church whose purpose it is to endorse and defend the status quo of some cultural identity, whether we call it the American Way, Western civilization, personal prosperity, or any other cultural norm. This is the church which has bowed her knee to Caesar and become a puppet of the very kinds of powers and principalities which God's kingdom stands against.

We also have the church of people-pleasing consumerism, whose way of life is driven by market calculations and whose philosophy is taken more from Wall Street than the word. This church's main goal is to continually propagate and expand itself organizationally without ever getting around to actually carrying out the mission to which the church was called. Like a virus, its main function is to take resources and reproduce without actually producing fruit of lasting value.

Then there are the churches which have embraced their mission but have misunderstood it. There is the church whose purpose is to preach the gospel of the get-out-of-jail-free card. It sees the gospel as just a contract for escaping hell, not an invitation to understand and live one's life on the basis of a new relation to God and one another through Christ. On the other hand, there is the church which preaches a gospel of mere humanitarianism. Here the church becomes just a means to an end; just another group seeking to make the world a better place on an ultimately humanistic foundation.

This is only a brief sampling, but sufficient to see how in so many ways churches have settled for a lesser vision of Christianity than what Paul has described and Christ has given. What all the above examples have in common is either implicitly or explicitly making Christianity a means to an end (whether of propping up a cultural status quo, maintaining a successful and popular organization, avoiding torment in the afterlife, or making this world a better place) rather than seeing it as an end in itself. If in fact Christianity is the fulfillment of God's creation-purposes in Christ, then it is intrinsically worthwhile. In that case, the church, which is the fellowship of those who share membership in God's kingdom and enjoy union with Christ the King, has a mission which is inseparable from its very existence. The church is not something created by humans for purposes we find valuable; it is a transformative reality created by God in Christ in which we dwell by faith and the power of the Holy Spirit.

But such dwelling is not passive. It means actively inhabiting the world as a certain kind of person formed by God; or better, as a community of such persons. We are to be the kinds of persons, and the kind of community, whose very existence and way of life together is an act of discipling the nations. This does not mean that we neglect the explicit proclamation of the gospel, but quite the opposite: it means that we are a people with the kind of self-understanding and pattern of life in which gospel proclamation is the logically consistent outcome. It means that by being rooted in Christ's love, we know who we are, where we come from, and where we are going. It means we are self-conscious inhabitants of a story that is older than creation itself and whose ending has already been written by the death and resurrection of Christ. To be such a person, to know ourselves as such, and to be willing to tell the truth, is to be a preacher of the gospel.

The bottom line is that Christian existence—as a people who are the fulfillment of God's creation purposes through union with Christ—is an intrinsically worthy one. It is not a tool for accomplishing something else (although whether it bears fruit is a valid test of its authenticity). It is an end in itself. Here we encounter the first and highest calling there is: to enter the fold of trinitarian love and the eternal worship of the living God.

But of course, this is a scandalous existence. It calls us to identify ourselves and to understand the world according to a different set of norms than those which are promoted according to the status quo. To be a Christian in the world is to love the world precisely by loving God supremely. We serve the world by being set apart from it as servants of the self-sacrificial savior. Our lives become an echo of the way in which God loves the world precisely in his being transcendent above it. Here we are reminded of the heartbeat of reality itself, which lives in the trinitarian rhythm of union and distinction. That is not only the rhythm by which God dances, but by which all relationships dance. By giving ourselves to God and one another, we affirm that which we were created to be. We affirm the circle of fellowship which is God's new creation in Christ: his church. We affirm the wisdom of God. We affirm reality itself.

CONCLUSION

But this requires courage. Will we stand in the power of Christ against the powers of darkness? Will we take up his cross as the banner of our victory over them? In the midst of a throng of deities clamoring for our allegiance, will we worship and serve God alone? Will our everyday lives, in each task and relationship, sing the praise of his glorious grace? In the midst of this world, will we be the people of God in Christ through his Spirit—a holy and scandalous people?

Bibliography

Aristotle. *Ethics*. In *The Philosophy of Aristotle*, translated by J. L. Creed and A. E. Wardman, 334. New York: Signet, 2011.
Augustine. *Confessions*. Translated by Henry Chadwick. Oxford World's Classics. Oxford: Oxford University Press, 2009.
Barth, Karl. *The Epistle to the Romans*. Oxford: Oxford University Press, 1968.
Brunner, Emil. *The Mediator: A Study of the Central Doctrine of the Christian Faith*. Translated by Olive Wyon. Philadelphia: Westminster, 1947.
Buber, Martin. *I and Thou*. Translated by Walter Kaufmann. New York: Touchstone, 1971.
Carpenter, Micah. *Theology in the Second Person: The Contribution of Martin Buber's Dialogical Personalism To Evangelical Theological Method*. Unpublished Thesis submitted to Dr. David K. Clark. St. Paul: Bethel Seminary, 2019.
Cone, James. *Black Theology and Black Power*. Maryknoll: Orbis, 1997.
Fischer, Austin. *Young, Restless, No Longer Reformed: Black Holes, Love, and a Journey in and out of Calvinism*. Eugene, OR: Cascade, 2014.
Foster, Richard. *Celebration of Discipline*. New York: Harper Collins, 1988.
Fredrikson, Dean W. *Creation and Creation's God: One God, One Story, One People*. Denver: Outskirts, 2014.
Gutierrez, Gustavo. *A Theology of Liberation*. Maryknoll: SCM, 1988.
Hustad, Donald P., ed. *The Worshipping Church*. Carol Stream, IL: Hope Publishing, 1990.
Keller, Timothy. *The Prodigal God*. New York: Penguin, 2011.
Kierkegaard, Soren. *Purity of Heart Is to Will One Thing*. Translated by Douglass V. Steere. New York: Harper & Row, 1948.
King, Martin Luther, Jr. *The Autobiography of Martin Luther King Jr*. Edited by Clayborne Carson. New York: Warner, 2001.
Lewis, C. S. "The Apologist's Evening Prayer." In *Poems*, edited by Walter Hooper, 129. London: Bles, 1964.
———. *Mere Christianity*. New York: Harper Collins, 1952.
———. *The Screwtape Letters*. New York: Harper Collins, 1996.
Luther, Martin. "A Mighty Fortress Is Our God." In *The Worshipping Church*, edited by Donald P. Hustad, no. 43. Carol Stream, IL: Hope Publishing, 1990.
Peckham, John. *The Love of God: A Canonical Model*. Downers Grove: InterVarsity, 2015
Plato. *The Republic*. Translated by Desmond Lee. New York: Penguin, 2007.
Qureshi, Nabeel. *Seeking Allah, Finding Jesus: A Devout Muslim Encounters Christianity*. Grand Rapids: Zondervan, 2016.

Bibliography

Reuschling, Wyndy Corbin. *Reviving Evangelical Ethics: The Promises and Pitfalls of Classic Models of Morality*. Grand Rapids: Brazos, 2008.

Tayler, Charles. *A Secular Age*. Harvard: Belknap, 2007.

Vanhoozer, Kevin J. *The Drama of Doctrine: A Canonical-Linguistic Approach to Christian Theology*. Louisville: Westminster John Knox, 2005.

Wesley, Charples. *And Can It Be that I Should Gain*. In *The Worshipping Church*, edited by Donald P. Hustad, no. 473. Carol Stream, IL: Hope Publishing, 1990.

Wilsey, John. *American Exceptionalism and Civil Religion: Reassessing the History of an Idea*. Downers Grove: InterVarsity, 2015.

Wright, N. T. *Justification: God's Plan and Paul's Vision*. Downers Grove: InterVarsity, 2009.

www.ingramcontent.com/pod-product-compliance
Lightning Source LLC
Chambersburg PA
CBHW050807160426
43192CB00010B/1671